SELF-LEARNING MANAGEMENT SERIES

PUBLIC SPEAKING ESSENTIALS

YOU ALWAYS WANTED TO KNOW

Master confidence, storytelling, and audience engagement to deliver presentations that truly inspire.

AMI VED

PUBLIC SPEAKING ESSENTIALS
YOU ALWAYS WANTED TO KNOW

First Edition

Published by Vibrant Publishers LLC, USA, www.vibrantpublishers.com

Paperback ISBN 13: 978-1-63651-635-6
Ebook ISBN 13: 978-1-63651-636-3
Hardback ISBN 13: 978-1-63651-637-0

Library of Congress Control Number: 2025945479

This publication is designed to provide accurate and authoritative information regarding the subject matter covered. The Author has made every effort in the preparation of this book to ensure the accuracy of the information. However, information in this book is sold without warranty, either expressed or implied. The Author or the Publisher will not be liable for any damages caused or alleged to be caused either directly or indirectly by this book.

All trademarks and registered trademarks mentioned in this publication are the property of their respective owners. These trademarks are used for editorial and educational purposes only, without intent to infringe upon any trademark rights. This publication is independent and has not been authorized, endorsed, or approved by any trademark owner.

Toastmasters International® and all other Toastmasters International trademarks and copyrights are the sole property of Toastmasters International. This book is the opinion of the author and is independent of Toastmasters International. It is not authorized by, endorsed by, sponsored by, affiliated with, or otherwise approved by Toastmasters International.

Vibrant Publishers' books are available at special quantity discounts for sales promotions, or for use in corporate training programs. For more information, please write to bulkorders@vibrantpublishers.com

Please email feedback/corrections (technical, grammatical, or spelling) to spellerrors@vibrantpublishers.com

Vibrant publishes in a variety of print and electronic formats and by print-on-demand. Some material included with standard print versions of this book may not be included in e-books in print-on-demand. To access the complete catalog of Vibrant Publishers, visit www.vibrantpublishers.com

Exclusive Online Resources for You

As our valued reader, your purchase of this book includes access to exclusive online resources designed to enhance your learning experience. These resources can be downloaded from our website, www.vibrantpublishers.com, and are created to help you apply public speaking concepts effectively.

Online resources for this book include the following:

1. Confident affirmations worksheet
2. SMART communication goal handbook
3. Leadership storytelling tools
4. Voice modulation exercises for corporates

Why are these online resources valuable:

- **Confidence reinforcement:** The confident affirmations worksheet provides daily affirmations to strengthen self-belief and support personal growth.
- **Goal-oriented progress:** The SMART communication goal handbook combines affirmations with structured goal sheets to keep your improvement measurable and focused.
- **Engaging delivery:** Leadership storytelling tools offer proven techniques to craft compelling stories that connect and hold audience's attention.
- **Professional presence:** Voice modulation exercises for corporates help you use tone, pitch, and pace effectively to deliver with authority and impact.

How to access your online resources:

1. **Visit the website:** Go to www.vibrantpublishers.com
2. **Find your book:** Navigate to the book's product page via the "Shop" menu or by searching for the book title in the search bar.
3. **Request the resources:** Scroll down to the "Request Sample Book/Online Resource" section.
4. **Enter your details:** Enter your preferred email ID and select "Online Resource" as the resource type. Lastly, select "user type" and submit the request.
5. **Check your inbox:** The resources will be delivered directly to your email.

Alternatively, for quick access: simply scan the QR code below to go directly to the product page and request the online resources by filling in the required details.

Happy learning!

SELF-LEARNING MANAGEMENT SERIES

TITLE	PAPERBACK* ISBN

BUSINESS AND ENTREPRENEURSHIP

Title	ISBN
BUSINESS COMMUNICATION ESSENTIALS	9781636511634
BUSINESS ETHICS ESSENTIALS	9781636513324
BUSINESS LAW ESSENTIALS	9781636511702
BUSINESS PLAN ESSENTIALS	9781636511214
BUSINESS STRATEGY ESSENTIALS	9781949395778
ENTREPRENEURSHIP ESSENTIALS	9781636511603
INTERNATIONAL BUSINESS ESSENTIALS	9781636513294
PRINCIPLES OF MANAGEMENT ESSENTIALS	9781636511542

COMPUTER SCIENCE AND TECHNOLOGY

Title	ISBN
BLOCKCHAIN ESSENTIALS	9781636513003
CYBERSECURITY ESSENTIALS	9781636514888
MACHINE LEARNING ESSENTIALS	9781636513775
PYTHON ESSENTIALS	9781636512938

DATA SCIENCE FOR BUSINESS

Title	ISBN
BUSINESS ANALYTICS ESSENTIALS	9781636514154
BUSINESS INTELLIGENCE ESSENTIALS	9781636513362
DATA ANALYTICS ESSENTIALS	9781636511184

FINANCIAL LITERACY AND ECONOMICS

Title	ISBN
COST ACCOUNTING & MANAGEMENT ESSENTIALS	9781636511030
FINANCIAL ACCOUNTING ESSENTIALS	9781636510972
FINANCIAL MANAGEMENT ESSENTIALS	9781636511009
MACROECONOMICS ESSENTIALS	9781636511818
MICROECONOMICS ESSENTIALS	9781636511153
PERSONAL FINANCE ESSENTIALS	9781636511849
PRINCIPLES OF ECONOMICS ESSENTIALS	9781636512334

*Also available in Hardback & Ebook formats

SELF-LEARNING MANAGEMENT SERIES

TITLE	PAPERBACK* ISBN

HR, DIVERSITY, AND ORGANIZATIONAL SUCCESS

TITLE	PAPERBACK* ISBN
DIVERSITY, EQUITY, AND INCLUSION ESSENTIALS	9781636512976
DIVERSITY IN THE WORKPLACE ESSENTIALS	9781636511122
HR ANALYTICS ESSENTIALS	9781636510347
HUMAN RESOURCE MANAGEMENT ESSENTIALS	9781949395839
ORGANIZATIONAL BEHAVIOR ESSENTIALS	9781636512303
ORGANIZATIONAL DEVELOPMENT ESSENTIALS	9781636511481

LEADERSHIP AND PERSONAL DEVELOPMENT

TITLE	PAPERBACK* ISBN
DECISION MAKING ESSENTIALS	9781636510026
INCLUSIVE LEADERSHIP ESSENTIALS	9781636514765
INDIA'S ROAD TO TRANSFORMATION: WHY LEADERSHIP MATTERS	9781636512273
LEADERSHIP ESSENTIALS	9781636510316
TIME MANAGEMENT ESSENTIALS	9781636511665

MODERN MARKETING AND SALES

TITLE	PAPERBACK* ISBN
CONSUMER BEHAVIOR ESSENTIALS	9781636513263
DIGITAL MARKETING ESSENTIALS	9781949395747
MARKETING MANAGEMENT ESSENTIALS	9781636511788
MARKET RESEARCH ESSENTIALS	9781636513744
MODERN ADVERTISING ESSENTIALS	9781636514857
SALES MANAGEMENT ESSENTIALS	9781636510743
SERVICES MARKETING ESSENTIALS	9781636511733
SOCIAL MEDIA MARKETING ESSENTIALS	9781636512181

*Also available in Hardback & Ebook formats

SELF-LEARNING MANAGEMENT SERIES

TITLE	PAPERBACK* ISBN
OPERATIONS MANAGEMENT	
AGILE ESSENTIALS	9781636510057
OPERATIONS & SUPPLY CHAIN MANAGEMENT ESSENTIALS	9781949395242
PRODUCT MANAGEMENT ESSENTIALS	9781636514796
PROJECT MANAGEMENT ESSENTIALS	9781636510712
STAKEHOLDER ENGAGEMENT ESSENTIALS	9781636511511

CURRENT AFFAIRS

DIGITAL SHOCK	9781636513805

*Also available in Hardback & Ebook formats

About the Author

Ami Ved is a professional communication coach, keynote speaker, and soft skills expert, as well as the founder of SpeakWithAmee Training and Coaching Company. An ICF CCE-certified trainer with over 20 years of experience—including a transformative decade in China—she has empowered thousands of professionals and leaders to speak with confidence, clarity, and charisma.

Once a last-bencher in school, Ami felt nervous, unheard, and unsure of her voice. But a journey through call centers, corporate boardrooms, and global classrooms transformed her life. Her voice proved to be her most valued asset, leading to sales success, corporate training, and global recognition. From being rejected in multiple interviews to becoming a LinkedIn Top Voice 2024 and a multi-award-winning speaker, her story is a living example of how communication can change everything.

Through her signature programs—*Confident Speaker Blueprint* and *Communication Mastery for Working Professionals*—Ami has coached IT professionals, entrepreneurs, and senior leaders from Unilever, BNP Paribas, Saint-Gobain, Prodapt, and many more. Her unique methods, including SpeakFlowPro, Voice Yoga, and the JT Fluency Technique, help individuals overcome stage fear, structure their thoughts, and speak with impact.

After restarting her career following a sabbatical, Ami hosted her first public speaking workshop at a small IB school—a moment that reignited her mission: to help 100,000 individuals worldwide rise from silence to stage and build a 50-crore communication coaching movement.

She believes, *"Your voice is your superpower—and when you learn to use it well, the world listens."*

When she's not coaching or leading corporate workshops, Ami can be found speaking at Toastmasters, sharing tips on LinkedIn, reading, trekking, or building LEGO masterpieces with her son, Vraj.

This book is a tribute to the unheard, a guide to finding your voice, and a reminder that your message truly matters.

What Experts Say About This Book!

In her book, Public Speaking Essentials, professional speaker, coach and trainer Ami Ved provides a comprehensive volume on the skills necessary to excel in any speaking situation.

Her step-by-step guide covers the WHAT, WHY and HOW of public speaking. Ms. Ved offers the respected results of years of research, but she backs it up with the proven principles and practices that have served successful speakers for centuries.

This book examines the psychological, emotional, and physical aspects of public speaking, and it serves as a guide for anyone who feels challenged by the very thought of going on stage.

Public Speaking Essentials is a 'must-read' and deserves its place on the bookshelf of anyone who wishes to speak with confidence, clarity and conviction.

– Mark Brown, Certified Speaking Professional (CSP),
World Champion Public Speaker 1995

This is one of the most holistic books you will find on public speaking. Not only does this share Ami's own journey of becoming a confident speaker but also is a step-by-step guide on how anyone can become a confident public speaker. If you want to beat nerves and succeed in every speaking situation, this book is for you.

– Suman Kher, Founder, Soft Skills Studio

The wealth of knowledge, experience, and understanding shared in this book will help you become a master of public speaking for any scenario you may find yourself in.

– Joshua Burney, Public Speaking Coach, Spoken Solutions

What Experts Say About This Book!

This book is packed with information presented in a friendly and approachable manner. I appreciated the honesty of the author about her own initial struggles with public speaking, making this book a more relatable read coming from lived experience. Chapters end with a helpful summary and a quiz. Information covered includes everything from the history of public speaking to the importance of nonverbal communication and adaptability in different settings. Because there is so much information and context here, it's useful that the chapters are broken down into more navigable sections if the reader happens to be looking for more specific advice.
– Zaidee Everettc, Librarian, Harborside Library, Johnson's and Wales University (JWU)

As with most things in life, the key to successful public speaking is preparation. And in this book, Ami Ved provides you with public speaking essentials to make your next speech, meeting, or toast a success.
– John. D. Branch, PhD, EdD, DProf, Research fellow at William Davidson Institute, University of Michigan

If you've ever felt unheard when speaking or worried that you sound less confident than you are, this book is for you. It explains how to speak with authority and connect naturally with others, without sounding forced. Whether you are presenting to your team or handling conversations, you'll gain practical tools that work. For those wanting to boost confidence in meetings, build your credibility, and lead with presence, this book is a must. You'll find yourself nodding along, thinking, yes, I can do this!
– Angelique Hamilton, HR & Workplace Consultant

Table of Contents

Preface

I once sat in the last row of my classroom, nervous, unheard, and unsure of my voice. My journey took me through call centers, corporate boardrooms, and global classrooms, where I discovered a life-changing truth—my voice is my greatest asset. It opened doors to sales success, corporate training, and international recognition. I went from being rejected in over 100 interviews to training at top corporations, becoming a LinkedIn Top Voice 2024, and a multi-award-winning speaker. My story proves that when you own your voice, you change your life.

Speaking at an international speech contest taught me another truth: confidence is everything. Public speaking is the world's number one fear, and I saw it holding back even the most talented professionals. In every corporate session I led, I met brilliant people who struggled to express their ideas. Over the last 20 years, I have trained more than 10,000 IT professionals, college students, senior leaders, and executives in India and China, and one pattern became clear—everyone needs the ability to communicate with clarity, confidence, and impact.

I wrote this book for you—if you've ever felt nervous before speaking, stayed silent in meetings, or wished your words had more impact. This book will show you step by step how to overcome stage fright, build authentic confidence, and command attention in any room. Through practical exercises, proven techniques, and inspiring stories, you will learn to find your voice, structure your thoughts, and speak in a way that people listen to and remember.

If I could go from the last bench to the global stage, you can too. This book is your guide to turning your voice into your superpower—so the world finally hears your story!

How will this book help you succeed?

Public Speaking Essentials was crafted to be your step- by- step companion, blending proven frameworks, mindset tools, and hands- on exercises. Inside you will find:

- **Foundation modules** that reframe fear into fuel, using mindset shift techniques to quiet self-doubt.
- **Structured frameworks for speech preparation,** such as the PREP method and the What-How-Why (W-H-W) method, can help you gauge your audience and prepare impactful speeches.
- **Delivery drills** for projection and variety, and posture techniques for stage presence.

Each chapter ends with reflective summary points and quiz questions, ensuring you don't just read about the techniques—you internalize them.

The changing landscape of professional communication

The current digital period has transformed how we connect. Virtual meetings, recorded webinars, and hybrid events mean that your "stage" can span continents—and so can the distractions. Microphones, cameras, and time zones add new layers of complexity: you must engage through a screen as effectively as you would in a room full of people. Meanwhile, attention spans have never been shorter; you have seconds to hook your audience before their focus drifts.

At the same time, cultural diversity and remote collaboration demand adaptive communication styles. What resonates in Mumbai may differ in Singapore or San Francisco. This book equips you to read the room—whether physical or virtual—and tailor your tone, pace, and storytelling to connect across backgrounds. By blending speaking principles with modern best practices, you'll learn to own any format and engage every audience, wherever they're tuning in.

Acknowledgments

This book is more than words on paper—it is the voice of every moment I doubted myself and every person who believed in me when I couldn't.

To my late grandfather, "Dada (Mulchand Bhavsar)," who taught me the right values and believed that I have a great stage presence, and encouraged me in my speaking journey.

To my family—my parents, my in-laws, and my husband, Dhaval—thank you for being my constant support and giving me the courage to dream louder.

To my son, Vraj, you are my biggest inspiration and motivation to do better each day.

To my mentors and coaches from whom I learned public speaking, to every guide who lit a spark along the way—thank you for reminding me that impact starts with service and that my story matters.

To the world champion and mentor, Mark Brown, for generously giving his valuable time and participating in the interview featured in the last chapter of this book.

To my Toastmasters family, especially Powai Toastmasters— thank you for being the stage that shaped me, the community that uplifted me, and the family that clapped the loudest when I found my voice.

To every student, professional, leader, and dreamer I've had the privilege to coach, thank you for trusting me with your journey. Your breakthroughs inspired this book.

To my SpeakWithAmee community—your energy, your wins, and your messages fuel me daily. We are building more than confidence; we are building a movement.

To the entire team at Vibrant Publishers for constant support, patience, and motivation; without them, this book wouldn't be possible.

And lastly, this book is for the little girl in me who once stayed silent in the classroom.

May every reader of this book remember:
You don't have to be perfect to be powerful. You just have to start speaking.

With all my heart,
Ami Ved

Introduction to the Book

What will you gain from this book?

- A detailed understanding of the basics of public speaking.
- Lessons on how to master the techniques for preparing, refining, and delivering your speech.
- A thorough understanding of how to know your audience well and how you can create a lasting impression on them.
- Knowledge about the common challenges faced by public speakers and practical tips on how to overcome them.
- Step-by-step guide to growing professionally as a public speaker.

Public speaking has become a dynamic aspect of our daily life, whether you are a student, professor, sales trainer, politician, community organizer, fundraiser, corporate communication adviser, or motivational speaker. It is a highly sought-after skill that everyone aspires to develop to grow personally and professionally.

Despite the popularity of public speaking, there are very few books that distinctly provide detailed steps for developing one's public speaking skills. This book, Public Speaking Essentials You Always Wanted to Know, is designed to help you, readers, understand the basics of public speaking. By going through its pages, you will discover some proven techniques for preparing, refining, and delivering your speeches. You will also discover the best approaches for identifying your target audience and preparing speeches that meet their needs. Public speaking presents inherent challenges, but this book addresses them, offering practical actions that you can take immediately to become a great public speaker.

Like many of you, the author went through periods of personal and professional development before she became the world-class speaker/corporate trainer that she is today. She documents her formative experiences in this book and provides useful pieces of advice for aspiring speakers who want to excel in the art of public speaking.

You don't have to grow alone as a speaker; therefore, see this book as a much-needed companion that offers step-by-step guidelines about how you can go from a novice to becoming a world-class public speaker. Your development as a speaker demands a certain level of seriousness on your part. This entails that by exploring this book chronologically, you will be able to see how the important skills for public speaking are described in order of significance, from identifying your purpose to specializing in a particular aspect of public speaking, whether as a motivational speaker, corporate trainer, entertainer, or university professor. You will discover all the necessary tools of the public speaking trade in the book.

Do you know that a powerful speech involves storytelling, incorporating personal anecdotes, and utilizing communication tools such as visual aids and nonverbal communication cues? You will unearth all these nuggets of wisdom or knowledge about the speaking profession from *Public Speaking Essentials You Always Wanted to Know.*

Good luck with the amazing discoveries awaiting you in the book!

Who Can Benefit From This Book?

Public speaking is a much-sought-after skill in the sense that it is an integral aspect of communication. Unfortunately, not everyone is capable of delivering an impromptu speech, a corporate training, or a conversation in a family meeting, or even having a friendly discussion with associates or friends. If you are in that situation, this book is specifically written to help you master public speaking, doing so with absolute ease if you can set aside time to learn the essential bits and pieces of public speaking described in it.

You can benefit immensely from this book if you are:

- An entrepreneur pitching an idea to investors concerning your potential company, products, or services.
- A professional seeking a promotion and advancement to a managerial position.
- A student giving a class presentation or aspiring to become a teacher, a community organizer, or a politician, etc.
- A parent inspiring your child to master the fundamentals of public speaking.
- A leader rallying a team toward a vision or goal, using the power of your voice to win their loyal followership.
- A person whose ambition is to become a professional and high-paying public speaker.

How to Use This Book?

This book was intentionally designed to be an interactive one, which means that you can easily discover any topic on public speaking by simply flipping to the appropriate chapters or pages that contain the exact information you are seeking.

Here is a list of the most common topics readers generally desire to have deep knowledge of, as far as public speaking is concerned:

1. **What are the basics of public speaking?** This requires understanding the evolution of public speaking, the striking differences between public speaking and conversation, and how to build confidence and overcome fear. If you are a student wishing to understand what speaking is all about or you are an aspiring public speaker, find out about the fundamentals of public speaking in Chapters 1 and 3 of the book.

2. **Preparing your speech:** You will need to identify your speech's purpose and audience by setting clear objectives and tailoring your message to different audiences. If you are a company trainer, an HR manager, or even a politician, you will be required to carefully prepare your speech before delivering it. See Chapter 2 for the best approach for preparing a powerful speech.

3. **How to structure your speech?** It starts with gathering reliable information for your speech in a way that informs, persuades, and motivates your audience. If you are a community leader, a graduate student defending your project, or a social commentator, Chapter 4 explains how you can properly structure your speech to excite your audience.

4. **The power of storytelling:** In public speaking, stories matter a lot. By incorporating the elements of a good story, such as personal anecdotes and analogies, you can successfully carry your audience along. Check out Chapters 5 and 6 for some effective techniques concerning the use of stories, anecdotes, and analogies to make your speeches memorable.

5. **The art of delivering your speech:** Using visual aids, statistics, and nonverbal cues effectively, and experimenting with diverse forms of speech delivery techniques, you can make a success of delivering a powerful and memorable speech. Whether you are an experienced public speaker, master of ceremonies, a school teacher, or a program coordinator, read from Chapter 7 to Chapter 11 to discover the most proactive manner to deliver speeches.

6. **Summarizing and ending the speech:** The ending of your speech must be as riveting as its beginning and middle. A poorly concluded presentation may leave a bad impression on your audience. For everyone desirous to be a great public speaker, Chapter 12 explains how you can end your speech on a high note.

By exploring *Public Speaking Essentials You Always Wanted To Know*, you will uncover more details about the above-mentioned topics and many more related ideas or concepts relating to public speaking.

CHAPTER 1

Understanding the Basics of Public Speaking

Key Learning Objectives

- Gain insights into the evolution of public speaking.
- Understand the difference between public speaking and conversation.
- Learn how to build confidence and overcome fear

When I was 10 years old, a teacher asked me to come to the front and speak, but I froze. Several years later, I walked into a meeting, and my boss requested that I lead the meeting, and I froze again.

Now, picture another scenario: You're at a family gathering trying to share an important decision, but no one seems to take you seriously. Or, you have a brilliant idea that could transform your business, yet when you present it to investors, your lack of confidence makes them hesitant to trust you.

Your ability to speak with confidence, clarity, and conviction can change the game for you.

1.1 The Evolution of Public Speaking

The history of public speaking dates back 2,500 years ago in ancient Athens (Greece) and Rome. In that period, the local officials, or men and women tasked with civic duties, were expected to deliver the progress of their works or assignments in elaborate public speeches.

Dr. Matt McGarrity, a lecturer at the Department of Communication, University of Washington, explained that *"A class on public speaking is, in essence, a class on rhetoric. So, what is rhetoric, according to McGarrity? The Greeks and Romans spent a lot of time thinking about what sounds good, what looks good, and what works well for an audience.*

Aristotle defined rhetoric as the faculty of discovering in any particular case the available means of persuasion. This is a very analytic definition. Plato held that "rhetoric is the art of winning the soul by discourse"—a very motivational definition. The contemporary writer, Gerard Hauser, defines rhetoric as communication that attempts to coordinate social action. Its goal is to influence human choices on specific matters that require immediate attention. That's a pretty pragmatic definition.

Rhetoric for us is about figuring out what needs to be communicated and then doing that well. It's about analyzing the situation you find yourself in and then using rhetorical tools to craft a strategic and effective response. Rhetoric is one of the ways we're going to study the art of public speaking. It's a useful tradition, and that's why it's been with us for over 2,500 years."[1]

Public speaking wasn't only a tool of communication for democratic or civic purposes; it gradually became a mode of communication in certain professions such as law, philosophy, and creative writing. It involved a group

---

1. Matt, McGarrity. "Introduction to Public Speaking (Coursera, 2025)",accessed 12 October, 2024, https://www.coursera.org/instructor/mcgarrity

of people gathering to listen to the motivating speeches of revered or well-respected lawyers, political activists, philosophers, creative writers, community leaders, etc.

Public speaking has also been featured prominently in religions—Christian Apostles like Peter and Paul have spoken boldly in front of people packed full in the Sanhedrin, synagogues, temples, and royal courts. Islamic scholars have been noticed addressing huge crowds in Mecca, Baghdad, Damascus, Tripoli, etc.[2]

Public speaking has also been used as a weapon of propaganda during the two World Wars. China, in particular, utilized public speaking to rally its over one billion people around its cultural insularity and strict communist ideologies.[3]

As demonstrated above, public speaking is a force of nature that can be put to either a good or evil use. When Martin Luther King, Jr.,[4] with popular and powerful speeches, mobilized the coloreds against every act of oppression in America, he was able to put the African Americans and other minorities on the path to lasting freedom. Similarly, Mahatma Gandhi's fiery anti-Britain rhetoric, "*Quit India movement speech* on '*Do or die,*'" eventually contributed to India's independence from the United Kingdom after over two hundred years.

On the other hand, political historians believed that the speech Adolf Hitler gave in the Kroll Opera House on 30th

---

2. John, Hale,*The Art of Public Speaking: Lessons From the Greatest Speeches in History (THE GREAT COURSES, 2010)*, 28-45.

3. Zhao Alexandre Huang,.*"China's Public Diplomacy and Confucius Institute". Public Diplomacy and the Politics of Uncertainty (2021)*:ff10.1007/978-3-030-54552-9_8ff. ffhal-02910002f

4. Martin Luther, King, Jr., *I Have a Dream: Writings and Speeches That Changed the World, Special 75th Anniversary Edition* (HarperOne, 2003), 56-88.

January 1939, to the Reichstag delegates, indicated that he pre-planned the Holocaust incident.[5]

Most especially in this modern, technologically advanced age, public speaking has gone beyond mere face-to-face conversations or discussions. Nowadays, speakers can reach millions of audiences from the comfort of their homes using laptops and smartphones. The digital age has tremendously transformed how we connect, share ideas, and interact with one another.

One of the most reputable, global platforms for public speakers' development is Toastmasters International. As a nonprofit organization, Toastmasters is reportedly over 100 years old, and it is operational in 127 countries.[6] I have been a proud member of this organization for the past seven years. I must confess that associating with it has positively impacted my communication and leadership skills, boosting my confidence more than ever before.

In this modern world, public speakers can reach a diverse audience in real-time via social media, well-structured webinars, and other online-based communities or avenues. The great thing about this approach is that it eliminates the vacuum and makes it possible for speakers to consistently get their important messages across to their excited audiences.

The TED conference is a typical example of how digital or online communication and face-to-face conversations can be combined to revolutionize the field of public speaking. Each speaker in a curated TED conference event has 18 minutes or less to deliver their powerful speech, and the audience size can range from 1,200 to 1,500 attendees. On the other

---

5. Der-Fuehrer, "Adolf Hitler-Speech to the Reichstag", Der-Fuehrer, accessed 20 November, 2024, *https://www.der-fuehrer.org/reden/english/34-07-13.htm*

6. "100 Years of Communication Excellence." Toastmasters International, accessed 10 December, 2024, https://www.toastmasters.org/

hand, TEDx events usually admit fewer attendees, usually about 100 people. However, there is no limit to a TEDx event if the audience is entirely online around the world. TED conferences are directly managed by TED itself, while TEDx events are planned and sponsored by local organizers without getting any financial assistance from TED.

Public speakers who have previously participated in TED conferences and TEDx events often attested to how the experience of participating in those events had significantly improved their personal branding and positively boosted their credibility. They are now mostly perceived by their audiences as knowledgeable public speakers who are worth listening to.

Both TED and TEDx can reach millions of audiences across the globe. It is estimated that in 2012, TED and TEDx videos surpassed over one billion views and streams.[7]

1.2 Public Speaking vs. Conversation

It is said that both public speaking and conversation are means of communication. The main differentiating factors between public speaking and conversation are that the former is well-structured, mostly formal, and is usually properly delivered, while conversation can be mostly informal, not usually structured, and it is often a result of interactions between two people or more.

In today's world, public speaking is part of our education, business, and political communication strategy. Regularly, lectures are organized in schools, religious places, private avenues, and public spaces to create awareness about important issues and/or promote certain ideas.

---

7. "TED reaches its billionth video view!", TED Blog, accessed 4 May, 2025, https://blog.ted.com/ted-reaches-its-billionth-video-view/

On the other hand, conversations can occur between two or more friends, classmates, colleagues, neighbors, and acquaintances. Conversations can be part of public speaking platforms, and the conversational way of public speaking creates a greater impact and community-building.

Public speaking usually involves a larger audience when compared to conversations. The size of the audience can range from ten people to tens of thousands of participants or attendees. However, a couple of friends or more may engage in conversations, and they are not expected to hold one another to a high standard in the areas of planning, development, and delivery of their communication. This indicates that a conversation may be about anything—any topic of interest shared by those involved in it.

Figure 1.1 **Types of Public Speaking**

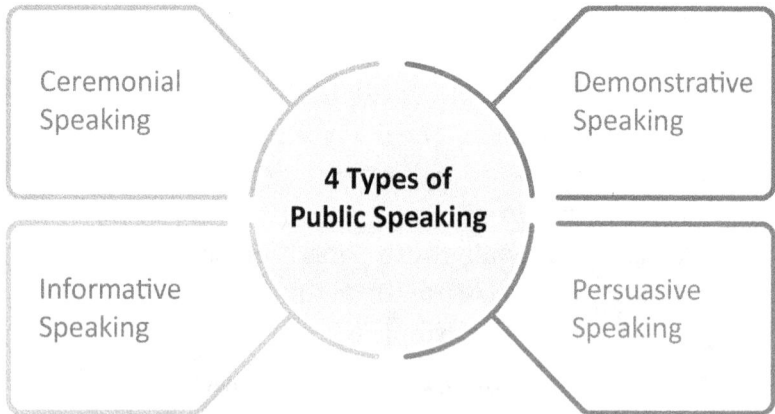

(Adapted from CBitss Technology, 2025)[8]

---

8. "Different Types of Public Speaking", CBitss Technologies, accessed 10 September, 2024, https://www.slideshare.net/slideshow/different-types-of-public-speaking/220683508

Public speaking comes in different forms, but there are four main types, which are described in detail below:

1. **Ceremonial speaking:** Ceremonial speaking is usually employed in parties, social gatherings, award-presentation events, and so on. For example, Lebron James, during the 2023 ESPYS, hosted at the Dolby Theatre in Los Angeles on July 12, 2023, gave a fascinating speech about his commitment to basketball when he was awarded the Best Record-Breaking Performance.[9]

2. **Persuasive speaking:** As its name implies, persuasive speaking aims at persuading people to take action; they may not necessarily be members of the public. For example, Martin Luther King's *"I Have a Dream"*, a speech he delivered on August 28, 1968, rallied African Americans to seek an end to racism and anti-minority policies in America. In a movie titled "Braveheart (1995)", the Scottish nationalist, William Wallace (played by Mel Gibson) urged Scottish men and women to take up arms and risk their lives, limbs, and vital organs to fight for their freedom.

   Usually, a persuasive speech intends to incite the audience to take some tangible actions or to willingly accept an ideology aimed at addressing certain aspects of their humanity. Teachers can also deliver persuasive speeches to encourage their students to do their best in their studies.

3. **Informative speaking:** This kind of communication provides much-needed information about something, people, or activities. A company may utilize informative speaking at expositions or conferences to

---

9. Lebron James, *"LeBron James Says He Can Still Give the Game Everything"*, YouTube, 5:36, https://www.youtube.com/watch?v=YonmfL9GvOw

tell great stories about their existing or new products/ services.

4. **Demonstrative speaking:** This is used to illustrate or demonstrate something in a vivid way that will make it memorable and understandable. For instance, a professor may decide to use demonstrative speaking to explain a principle or an idea. A typical form of demonstrative speaking is the "show and tell method," which is the practice of showing something to an audience and describing it to them, usually with a toy or other children-oriented items. Children learn a lot of things during their first stage of speech through demonstrative speaking.

Other kinds of public speaking include:

5. **Motivational speaking:** The purpose of motivational speaking is to use words or communication to motivate or energize certain groups of people. They could be students, employees, or members of the same association, club, or political party.

6. **Impromptu:** This is a speech or a form of speaking that is delivered without prior planning and preparation. When someone is suddenly asked to deliver a speech in public, that is referred to as an impromptu speech. Many candidates who go for job interviews in sales and customer service are asked to give impromptu speeches as well.

7. **Entertaining speaking:** People can deliver short and interesting speeches at places of entertainment such as nightclubs, bars, etc. Standup comedy is the best example of entertaining speeches. There has been a growing interest in standup comedy among American youths, powered by the ever-expanding catalog of Netflix standup comedy specials. Recently, John

Mulaney's "*Baby J*" was very popular among young people in America.

8. **Special occasion speeches:** Special occasions such as weddings, commencement, housewarming, etc., may require delivering a short and engaging speech.

1.3 Building Confidence and Overcoming Fear

Public speaking is a daunting task for many, often stirring a deep sense of fear and anxiety. The idea of standing before an audience and delivering a presentation can be so overwhelming that it becomes a source of significant stress.

I still remember how a 12-year-old me went to the stage for an elocution competition at school and was stammering all the time. Later, this happened when I had to do presentations with my senior leaders during sales presentations. I was consumed by dread. My words stumbled, my face flushed, and I wished desperately to escape. My subconscious inner critic thrived in those moments, and I felt my credibility slip away.

It was never one of my wildest future dreams that 18 years later, public speaking would be a regular part of my job as a corporate trainer. Despite ample practice, with sleepless nights, each speaking engagement is still nerve-racking for me. Whenever I sign up to present to a particular audience, initial excitement gradually morphs into anxiety and impostor syndrome. As the day approaches, I usually find myself pacing, rehearsing aloud, and worrying about my delivery. The night before, my sleep is commonly interrupted by constant waking, driven by anticipation and fear of oversleeping.

On the day of the presentation, I normally have butterflies in my stomach, and I sometimes question myself: "Why did I agree to this?"

Has that ever happened to you? Does this sound familiar?

Public speaking ranks among the most common fears globally, affecting 72%–75% of the population, according to Google.[10]

Fear of public speaking is called Glossophobia. This fear surpasses that of death, heights, and spiders. Several factors contribute to this anxiety.

In his submission, Dr. Michael DeGeorgia[11] of Case Western University Hospital explained that the prefrontal lobes of the human brain arrange our memories, and it is quite sensitive to anxiety. According to him, *"If your brain starts to freeze up, you get more stressed and the stress hormones go even higher. That shuts down the frontal lobe and disconnects it from the rest of the brain. It makes it even harder to retrieve those memories."*

This explains why people suffering from acute glossophobia often turn into stammerers on the stage. They are usually covered with sweat and experience a fast heartbeat as they struggle to remember everything they had memorized while preparing for their speech. Other symptoms associated with glossophobia include, but are not limited to, heart palpitations, stomach cramps, dry mouth, cold, sweaty palms, shaking voice, and shaky hands.

---

10. "Public Speaking: Getting beyond the fear through the three P's", University of Florida (IFAS Extension), accessed 5 February, 2025.https://blogs.ifas.ufl.edu/orangeco/2022/01/21/public-speaking-getting-beyond-the-fear-through-the-three-ps/

11. Michael, DeGeorgia, "Public Speaking Anxiety," *National Social Anxiety Center*, March 19, 2021.https://nationalsocialanxietycenter.com/social-anxiety/public-speaking-anxiety/#:~:text=The%20fear%20of%20public%20speaking%20is%20the%20most,fear%20is%20judgment%20or%20negative%20evaluation%20by%20others.

1.3.1 How to Overcome the Fear of Public Speaking

| Figure 1.2 | Tips and strategies to overcome the fear of public speaking. |

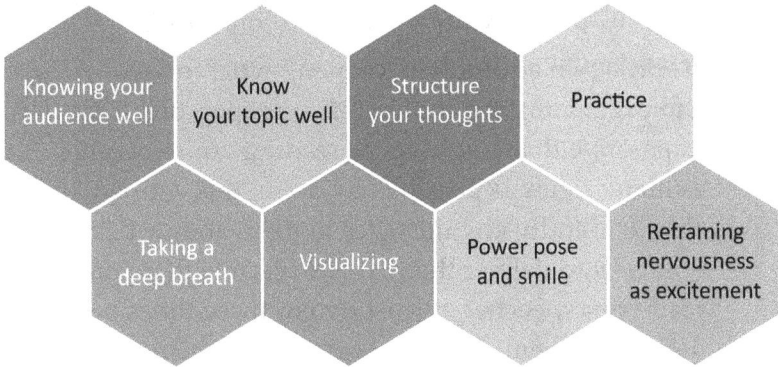

(Adapted from Teachthought, 2025)[12]

If you are affected by glossophobia or have some fear about public speaking, you can increase your confidence level by:

1. **Knowing your Audience:** Understand who you're presenting to, and what they hope to gain. Consider the impression you want to leave.

2. **Knowing your topic well:** Mastering your topic or subject matter can help you overcome the initial fear that often hits speakers' minds when appearing in front of an audience, small or big. Realizing that you have the necessary skills or experience to deliver a speech about a topic can be helpful in encouraging you to "face your fear".

---

12. "10 Tips and strategies to overcome the fear of public speaking.", Teach Thought, accessed January 12, 2025, https://www.teachthought.com/education/5-quotes-to-help-overcome-the-fear-of-public-speaking/

3. **Structuring your thoughts:** Public speaking requires being intentionally organized—you need to properly outline and arrange your thoughts in a way that makes a lot of sense to your audience. The audience naturally responds in a positive manner to speeches that are sensible, properly organized, and impactful.

4. **Practicing:** In addition to knowing what to say and organizing the content of your speeches, it is imperative that you practice reading your speeches as many times as possible. By doing this, you will be able to identify any mistakes in them and/or discover how best to deliver them. It is advisable that you read your speeches at least two or three times before delivering them. As the adage goes, *"Practice brings about perfection!"* I often practice in *front* of the mirror or video record my speech and pay close attention to my timing.

5. **Taking a deep breath:** Experienced public speakers understand the importance of taking a deep breath while delivering a speech. It gives them time, no matter how little, to bring forth ideas stored in their memories. It also allows them the unique opportunity to scan the audience and gauge their reactions to their speeches. Embracing a moment of silence is a technique utilized by public speakers, and they sometimes use this opportunity to encourage contributions from their audiences. Experienced public speakers understand that interactive audiences will always take advantage of such moments of silence to say something back to the speakers, keeping the rapport as engaging and entertaining as expected.

   Taking a deep breath can be short, but speakers need to focus primarily on their breath while doing so. Deep breathing calms the body and mind. It is advisable that speakers should try box breathing while delivering their speeches: This involves inhaling for four seconds, holding their breath for four seconds, exhaling for four seconds, and holding for another four seconds. Then repeat this procedure four times.

It is important to consider the usefulness of both the stepwise and pointwise approaches as far as taking a deep breath is concerned:

A. Stepwise approach:

- **Before the speech:** Practice deep belly breaths to maximize your lung capacity while supporting your voice. You also need to engage in meditation or mindfulness to calm your nerves during this period.

- **During the speech:** Plan to take a deep breath after sentences or long clauses. Avoid shallow breathing and quickly recover from nervousness by momentarily having a pause and taking two deep, slow breaths.

B. Pointwise Approach: Undertake the following steps to fully achieve a pointwise deep breathing technique:

- Whenever possible, breathe through your nose (nasal breathing); this kind of breathing warms and filters your vocal cords with air.

- Do not fill your lungs with a lot of air, as this could lead to difficulty breathing and tension in your body.

- To facilitate easier breathing, relax your shoulders and neck.

- Use pauses to add dramatic effect to your speech.
- Do the above-mentioned procedures regularly.

6. **Visualizing:** It is not every time a public speaker will have enough time to plan, organize, and practice their speeches. For example, when delivering an impromptu speech, it is quite helpful to rely on visualization, which involves putting whatever one aims to say to the public in pictures. By creating these vivid pictures in their minds, public speakers can hold their audiences spellbound for several hours. Speakers should visualize success like athletes, who often mentally prepare themselves for victory by visualizing a successful presentation and positive audience reactions.

Usain Bolt, the well-decorated Jamaican Olympic runner, who happened to be the only person alive to have won 100m and 200m gold medals in three consecutive Olympics (2008, 2012, and 2016), claimed that he used visualization to run his races and win even before those races were officially started.

David McCandless, a popular 21st-century TED speaker, uses visualization tools like infographics to create vivid and memorable elements of his speech in what can be described as a typical "See It, Say It, and Do It" methodology.[13]

If you face fears, keep some pointers in mind and use abbreviations to streamline your speech delivery. Use anecdotes, if needed.

---

13. "David McCandless draws beautiful conclusions from complex datasets — thus revealing unexpected insights into our world", *TED, accessed May 10, 2025,* https://www.ted.com/speakers/david_mccandless

Any speaker who is struggling with memorizing some parts of his/her speech can systematically switch his/her brain to the facts already researched, documented, and organized about the topic and use those facts to overcome his/her fear.

7. **Power Pose and Smile:** Before presenting, speakers should adopt a power pose and smile. Expanding your body and projecting confidence can help ease nerves and enhance self-assurance.

   Here are two simple body hacking tricks usually employed in public speaking:

   A. The Winner's V: This was discovered by researchers who studied people throughout the world after winning some big events they participated in. In the picture below, I was so excited after completing a 120km Biking Race that I had this pose.

Figure 1.3 Author posing in the winner's V pose

All winners, from global sportsmen and sportswomen who triumphed in the Olympic Games to the Indian cricket team winning the World Cup, display the same body language after victory. They stand up tall and throw their arms in a strong, high V shape.

However, you don't actually have to win any trophy or race before applying the benefits of the Winner's V pose as part of your lifestyle or while delivering your speeches. Just stand tall and put your hands in a V shape before that presentation or public speaking, and count 10 seconds, the longer the better. People do this before a strategic executive meeting in a bathroom. They get that immediate confidence and smile. I often do this before standing in front of a large audience, and I usually get a dose of confidence chemical immediately generated in my brain.

B. **The Superhero stance:** It shows assertiveness in communication. Stand tall and imagine that you are Batman or Wonder Woman, who became rich after a day's hard work, rather than fighting evil all night. Hands on hips, shoulders back, chest proud, and chin up. You can do this in any private space, and it will definitely give you confidence or a boost.

| Figure 1.4 | Superhero stance |

Both poses are body-hacking tools for winners, and they can make you feel more confident before appearing on the stage.

8. **Reframe Nervousness as Excitement:** It is advisable that speakers should reframe their mindsets from "I'm so nervous" to "I'm so excited." This positive language can change energy channels constructively. Use affirmations and practice them regularly, more than a month before your speech. Here is an exercise: Write down 5 negative sentences that your mind speaks on a daily basis on a sheet of paper. Now, reframe these sentences from negative to positive. For example, from "I am scared of Public speaking" to "I enjoy public

speaking. Every day, my speaking skills are getting better and better."

Reframing means shifting the way you think about a situation so as to respond with more confidence, clarity, and control. It's not about denying reality—it's about choosing a more helpful perspective.

TIP

How to Reframe Your Thoughts in Public Speaking?

Public speaking isn't a test—it's a gift of value to your audience. Instead of thinking, "What if I mess up?" try these reframes:

☑ Reframe #1:

✘ "I'm nervous."

☑ "I'm excited to share something valuable."

☑ Reframe #2:

✘ "They're judging me."

☑ "They're here to learn from me."

☑ Reframe #3:

✘ "I need to be perfect."

☑ "I just need to be clear, real, and helpful."

When you reframe your mindset, your voice, body language, and message follow, as great public speaking begins with not just words, but the way you see yourself and your role.

Chapter Summary

- Public speaking has evolved over the past 2,500 years, from being utilized as a medium of instruction by the ancient Greek philosophers, scholars, and Roman politicians to this present age, where it is primarily employed as a means of intellectual and creative communication or interaction.

- Public speaking is different from conversation in the sense that it involves speaking to a larger audience, using more structured and spontaneous language, and eliciting interactive responses from the audience. Conversation, on the other hand, is all about informal discussion between people who are friends, colleagues, and acquaintances, and it doesn't usually require structured language or a formal tone.

- The types of public speaking include but are not limited to motivational speaking, persuasive speaking, informative speaking, demonstrative speaking, impromptu, entertainment speaking, special occasion speeches, etc.

- To build confidence, public speakers need to know their audience well, deeply understand their topics, properly structure their thoughts, practice a lot, take deep breaths while speaking, visualize their messages, concentrate on facts and not fear, do a power pose, and reframe nervousness as excitement.

Quiz

1. The history of public speaking can be dated back to _____ years ago.
   a. 50
   b. 250
   c. 2500

2. The ancient Greek philosophers utilized public speaking as a vehicle for conveying their moralistic and instructional messages to their audiences.
   a. True
   b. False

3. Who published a treatise named "Rhetoric", highlighting the tactics that could be used in verbal persuasion?
   a. Socrates
   b. Aristotle
   c. The Roman Emperor

4. From the classical period, Renaissance period, and Industrial Revolution to the modern era, "Rhetoric" has been transferred in arrangement, delivery, effectiveness, and _____
   a. Rhyming
   b. Style
   c. Naming

5. One of the greatest, modern-day leaders who has utilized public speaking to transform their nation is _____

   a. Cicero
   b. Aristotle
   c. Mahatma Gandhi

6. The art of public speaking is NOT commonly applied in religions.

   a. False
   b. True

7. It was believed that Adolf Hitler's speech at the Kroll Opera House on 30 January 1939 was the precursor to the Holocaust. This demonstrated how public speaking is adopted for _____ cause.

   a. A religious
   b. An evil
   c. A good

8. Toastmasters International, which is a nonprofit organization, has a presence in 127 countries and was established over _____ years ago.

   a. 10
   b. 100
   c. 70

9. All of these are the main differences between a TED conference and a TEDx event except that _____ .
   a. A TED conference welcomes about 1200 attendees
   b. A TEDx is usually organized for a small, independent local audience
   c. Both a TED Conference and a TEDx are financially supported by TED

10. What separates public speaking from conversation is that _____ .
    a. It has a larger audience
    b. Its language is more structured and spontaneous
    c. It is an informal conversation between two or more friends

Answer Key

1 – c	2 – a	3 – b	4 – a	5 – c
6 – a	7 – b	8 – b	9 – c	10 – b

CHAPTER 2

Preparing Your Speech

Key Learning Objectives

- Identifying your purpose and audience
- Setting clear objectives
- Understanding your audience
- Tailoring your message to different audiences

Preparing a speech is like preparing dinner. There are some important thoughts we may have to struggle with, such as what kind of dinner are we going to cook? How do we cook it? What ingredients do we need to have ready before starting the cooking process? How do we properly input the right amount of ingredients into the dinner?

As revealed in Chapter 1, public speaking can be put to some good use, from being utilized in education to its adoption in business (corporate communication), entertainment, politics, religions, and lectures (for public awareness).

It is imperative for speakers to identify the specific purposes of their speeches and the categories of audience they will be addressing. Being equipped with these essential pieces of information will help speakers set clear objectives/goals and tailor their messages to meet their audiences' expectations.

2.1 Identifying Your Purpose and Audience

Every speaker, irrespective of their level of experience in public speaking, understands that they are invited to a conference or an event to deliver a particular message that will resonate with their audiences. This is why it is indispensable for speakers to identify the purpose of their speeches. They equally need to identify the nature of the audience they will be speaking to.

Let's explore the 5 Wives (5Ws) and 1 Husband (H) of speech-making:

- What is the purpose of your speech?
- Who is your audience?
- When is your speech (the date)?
- Where is your speech (the place)?
- Why do you need to prepare for the speech?
- How will you solve the jigsaw puzzle presented in your speech?

Your responses to the important questions above will help you complete the essential parts of your speech puzzles. In fact, you will be able to determine the beginning and end of your speech from the useful information gathered. More importantly, knowing the nature and purpose of your speech beforehand will empower you to create the most appropriate analogies you can use while delivering the speech. Remember to set intentions before you enter the room so that you know exactly what value to offer your audience.

2.2 Setting Clear Objectives

The following approaches can practically help speakers set achievable objectives or goals when called upon to undertake a speaking assignment:

2.2.1 Define your purpose

Taking the time to clearly define your purpose for each speech can go a long way to streamlining your delivery.

You need to properly provide an answer to these all-important questions:

1. What does your speech aim to achieve?
2. Is it to inspire your audience?
3. Is it to educate your audience?
4. Is it to persuade your audience, or is it to entertain your audience?

Here are examples of popular speeches delivered by business leaders like Bill Gates, Richard Branson, and Steve Jobs.

Bill Gates' popular TED talks include *"Innovation to Zero!"*, *"Teachers need real feedback,"* etc.[14]

Richard Branson's famous TEDx talk is about *"Second Chances"*.[15]

However, Steve Jobs' famous speech *"How to Live Before You Die"* was only featured on TED because he had never given a TED talk himself.[16]

---

14. "Bill Gates' TED Talks", TED 2022, accessed 15 May, 2025, https://www.ted.com/speakers/bill_gates
15. "Second Chances", TEDx 2015, YouTube, https://www.youtube.com/watch?v=F2dFiK3wkR
16. "Steve Jobs: How to Live Before You Die 2005 Speech (Full Transcript)", The Singju Post, accessed 10 April, 2025, https://singjupost.com/steve-jobs-how-to-live-before-you-die-2005-speech-full-transcript/

2.2.2 Set SMART Goals

SMART is an acronym for Specific, Measurable, Attainable, Relevant, and Time-bound.

Figure 2.1 SMART Goals

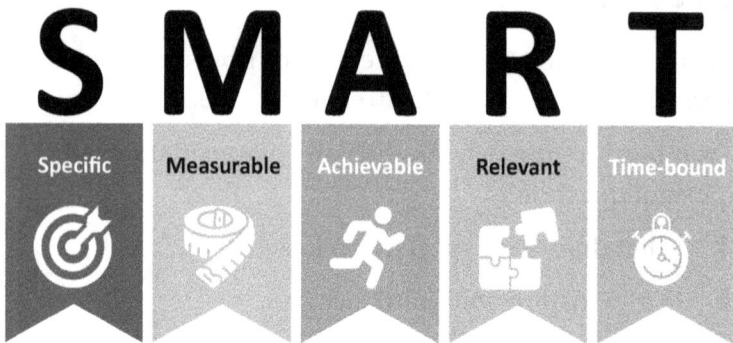

(Adapted from Virtual Orator, 2023)[17]

1. **Specific:** What specific goal would you like to achieve? For example, Avoid saying, "I want my audience to learn a lot from this speech," rather say, "I want them to discover some useful corporate communication strategies."

2. **Measurable:** How will you track your progress as a speaker? Will you time your practice sessions or get feedback after each speech? For example, "I will practice speaking for 15 minutes every day."

3. **Attainable:** Is this goal realistic based on your current speaking experience and time commitment? Set realistic goals that you can achieve.

4. **Relevant:** How does this goal align with your broader objective of becoming a more effective speaker? Ensure that your goals align with your overall speaking

---

17. "Creating SMART public speaking goals", Virtual Orator, accessed 10 September, 2024, https://virtualorator.com/blog/creating-smart-public-speaking-goals/

objectives. For example, saying, "I will listen to other great speakers' speeches every day" is relevant to improving your delivery style.

5. **Time-bound:** Make sure that you set a deadline for achieving that particular goal or objective.

2.3 Understanding Your Audience

Theodore Roosevelt, Jr., the 26th President of the United States, once said, *"Nobody cares how much you know, until they know how much you care!"* The main reason why speakers are often encouraged to understand their audience, like teachers, is to discover which weak areas their students need urgent strengthening or improvement.

Figure 2.2 The Perfect Speech Formula

Persuasion tactics · Storytelling · Body Language · Culture · YOU · YOUR AUDIENCE · PERFECTION · Nerves · Preparation · Tone of Voice · YOUR MESSAGE · Structure · Emotion

(Adapted from Speak With Persuasion. 2021)[18]

---

18. "The Perfect Speech Formula: What We Do (and Who We Do It for)", Speakwithpersuasion, accessed 5 September, 2024, The Perfect Speech Formula https://www.speakwithpersuasion.com/approach/

Typically, speakers need to familiarize themselves with their audiences' personal and professional needs to be able to accomplish the following purposes:

1. **To connect strongly with them** When you are invited to deliver a speech, it is just common sense to ask the organizers to provide adequate information about your intended audience. It pays to know their demographics, culture, expectations, and pain points so that you can prepare the exact messages that will strongly resonate with them. By using some appropriate examples, narratives, and topics that are mostly appealing to your audience, you will be able to connect with them on a personal level. They will genuinely appreciate your efforts in helping them overcome their challenges by providing much-needed encouragement or solutions in your messages.

   Charismatic global leaders often empathetically connect with their audience—be it at the local or international level—with the aim to achieve the greatest impact. They always research, prepare, and focus on the issues primarily affecting their audiences to catch their attention and connect with them.

   As a public speaker, to keep my audience glued to the core message that I want to deliver, I usually research my audience and their background, understanding their primary needs and concerns, and try to connect with them at ground level. This approach is always effective, because it makes them believe that I am there to genuinely help them and connect to their emotions.

   For example, while giving a keynote speech to Chinese students in one of the universities, I tried to learn some popular jargon and about the food that they served in the canteen. It was very easy for me to build rapport and connect with them.

2. **To have a great impact on them** Good speakers understand that it is not about the flowery language they use or their many years of experience in the speaking business, but it is about how much impact they can have on their audiences. In one of his talks, Simon Sinek describes his research findings concerning the significance of knowing one's "What", How", and "Why":

   A. **What?:** What is your speech about? What is its subject-matter?

   B. **How?:** How is your speech delivered? How does your audience prefer to be connected with? Face-to-face or online?

   C. **Why?:** Why are you delivering the speech? What is its primary purpose?

   As a speaker, you know you have greatly impacted your audience when they appear quite engaged with your materials, beaming with smiles, and being interactive, responding proactively to most of your prompts. Understanding the "why" of your speech can supercharge its delivery.

   On the other hand, a boring event can indicate two possibilities—it is either that the speaker is not good enough to smoothly carry the audience along, or the message isn't just right for them. In this case, the audience cannot clearly identify the "why" of the speech.

3. **For clarity** What do you think will happen when a university professor is sent to deliver a pep talk to a

group of elementary school students? There will be a disconnection between the speaker and the audience! If the professor lacks the capacity to simplify his message, the elementary school students will definitely be confused, not being able to understand anything the professor will be saying. In principle, for the audience to grasp the full scope of any message delivered by a speaker, it must be clear and understandable to them. Lack of clarity in speech delivery wastes everyone's time—both the speaker and the audience will feel unsatisfied after the speech, no matter how short or long it has been.

4. **For effectiveness** For a speech to be considered effective, it must have an immense impact on the audience to the extent that it produces certain feelings, which prompt them to take particular actions. However, nothing would have happened if the speech had been boring. What usually makes a speech dull is the lack of relatable stories, narratives, and examples that the audience can hang on to. On the contrary, utilizing engaging content and anecdotes can tremendously move the audience to respond emotionally to the message that is passed across to them.

5. **To be relevant** There is a chance that the message being delivered by the speaker may be totally irrelevant to the audience's requirements, or the speaker's knowledge may be below that expected by the audience. Asking a high-school graduate to speak to a group of engineers about how to do certain aspects of their job is a typical example of speaker-audience mismatch.

2.4 Tailoring Your Message to Different Audiences

Speaking to a single, uniform audience is easy, but unfortunately, that is usually not the case with public speaking. A uniform audience may consist of people who speak the same language, work in the same department within a company, or those in the same profession. In reality, speakers often find themselves addressing an audience composed of diverse people from different demographics, economic statuses, educational levels, and professional ranks.

The following tips will help you to properly tailor or customize your speech to meet the specific needs of your audience:

These are the five takeaways from Doumont's "Know Your Audience's Level of Expertise."[19]

1. **Avoid overexplaining to experts or overwhelming novices:** "The more your audience differs from you, the more effort you must invest in adapting to them." Great speakers put themselves in the shoes of their audiences and deliver exactly what they need.

2. **Define a Clear Core Message:** Don't say everything — say the one thing that matters most to them. "If they remember just one idea, what should it be?" Your core message, as a speaker, should be the unifying central idea that your presentation is all about.

3. **Match the Format to Their Preference:** Use visuals for engineers, narratives for executives, or direct outcomes for decision-makers. "Different audiences process information in different ways." It will be ineffective

---

19. Doumont, Jean-Luc,. *Trees, Maps, and Theorems: Effective Communication for Rational Minds.* (Principiae, 2009)

to use slides that contain complex jargon or business terminology for novices who cannot understand their meanings.

4. **Anticipate Objections and Questions:** Think ahead about what they may resist, challenge, or doubt, and address them upfront. "Effective communicators answer before being asked." More importantly, by getting to know your audience better, you will have identified what they like and what they do not approve of.

5. **Respect Their Time and Attention Span:** Be concise and focused. Less is more when you're audience-centered. "Cut what they don't need to hear—even if you love saying it." You don't necessarily have all the time in the world while delivering your speech; brevity always wins.

Chapter Summary

- As a speaker, you need to identify the purpose for which you are being invited to speak at a conference or an event. Is it to inform, motivate, demonstrate a skill, or just to entertain?

- Every seasoned speaker usually sets some specific goals or objectives they want to achieve in each of their speeches. By defining your speech purpose and setting SMART goals, a speaker can successfully inform, motivate, or entertain his or her audience.

- You should always endeavor to know your audience quite well so as to connect with them emotionally and intellectually. To do this, you first need to understand your audience's needs, preferences, pain points, cultures, and demographics.

- It is not every time that you will be speaking to an audience from the same demographic or social class; it is important that you tailor your speech to meet the requirements of all members of the audience if you happen to be speaking to a diverse audience. Otherwise, some members of the audience will be carried along while others will feel left behind.

Quiz

1. **What does the "S" in the acronym "SMART" goals stand for?**

    a. Scene

    b. Specific

    c. Students

2. **Is it always important for speakers to know the purpose of being invited to speak at an event?**

    a. Yes, it is.

    b. No, it isn't.

3. **To know the purpose of their speech, speakers should ask themselves this helpful question: "What does my speech aim to achieve?"**

    a. True

    b. False

4. **Two speakers have been invited to speak at the same conference. Speaker A learns about his audience demographic and outlines the most appropriate speech that will suit them. Speaker B doesn't care to know the kind of people he will be speaking to, and he doesn't even have time to prepare for his speech. Which of the two speakers demonstrates an enviable level of professionalism?**

    a. Speaker B

    b. Speaker A

5. Why are speakers advised to limit the use of metaphors in their speeches?

   a. To use expressions and words **that** their audience is familiar with
   b. To speak less
   c. To impress their audience

6. Speakers are often encouraged to pay serious attention to their body language when delivering their speeches to their diverse audiences because _____

   a. Using body language is a waste of time.
   b. They may be unknowingly offending some members of their audience.
   c. Good speakers don't utilize body language at all.

7. Why are speakers discouraged from using slangs and jargons in their speeches?

   a. Their audiences who don't know their meanings may be confused
   b. Some audiences don't like slangs
   c. Some audiences are fine with slangs and jargons

8. Speakers should exhibit a high level of cultural sensitivity when speaking to a diverse audience.

   a. False
   b. True

9. **For speakers, one of the merits of speaking naturally to their audiences is that** _____

    a. They can easily catch the message they are delivering.

    b. They can ask for an additional payment by using more time.

    c. They can speak to the audience as if they are speaking to babies.

10. **How do speakers ensure that their messages are relevant?**

    a. They need to first identify their audiences' requirements.

    b. They don't need to bother about what their audiences need.

    c. They should just deliver any messages they already have.

Answer Key

1 – b	2 – a	3 – a	4 – b	5 – a
6 – b	7 – a	8 – b	9 – a	10 – a

CHAPTER 3

Rhetoric and Canons of Rhetoric

Key Learning Objectives

- Introduce the concepts of rhetoric and canons of rhetoric
- Understand how to gather reliable information
- Learn how to organize your research
- Gain insights on the IPM (Inform, Persuade, Motivate) of speech

Rhetoric has been briefly mentioned in Chapter 1, but efforts are made in this chapter to broadly define the concept of "Rhetoric", explain its practical applications in speech-making, and describe what benefits public speakers stand to gain from having a deep understanding of rhetoric.

Most importantly, speakers can leverage their knowledge of rhetoric to gather proper information about their topics/themes and properly organize their findings to deliver high-impact, flawless, and memorable speeches.

3.1 Rhetoric and Canons of Rhetoric: An Introduction

Rhetoric is defined as the art of persuading others through communication; this can be done through a speech or in writing. There have been conflicting claims about the specific origin of rhetoric. However, it is indisputable that much of rhetoric, as a branch of the humanities, was advanced and developed by the ancient Greek philosophers. As a matter of fact, Plato coined the word "Rhetoric", and his disciple, Aristotle, prolifically published some notes on rhetoric and took it upon himself to explain, in some detail, the functional usage of the concept.[20]

It is generally believed that the ancient Greek philosophers had limited the scope of rhetoric only to political and civic uses. In other words, they mainly utilized the rhetorical technique to train high-class orators, lawyers, historians, poets, politicians, statesmen, etc. When it reached the Western world, rhetoric was applied in education and widely adopted as a useful persuasive technique in public discourse.

Those who disputed that rhetoric holistically originated from ancient Greece pointed out that there had been alternative but related techniques being used in persuasive speeches in places like Egypt, Mesopotamia, China, and South America even before the word rhetoric was invented.[21]

Aristotle deserves much credit for developing and expanding the Greek-originated rhetoric, which he had publicized in many of his publications. He once wrote that

---

20. Aristotle and Robert Bartlett, Aristotle's Art of Rhetoric (Chicago, Chicago University Press, 2021), 12-65.

21. Atilla Hallsby, "Chapter 2: The "Origins" of Rhetorical Theory," University of Minnesota Open Library, accessed October 7, 2024. https://open.lib.umn.edu/rhetoricaltheory/chapter/chapter-2/

"rhetoric is a combination of the science of logic and the ethical branch of politics." This entails that rhetoric provides a helpful tool for pragmatically solving issues with well-articulated arguments.

According to Aristotle, there are three intrinsic appeals of rhetoric to an audience: logos, pathos, and ethos.[22] Logos, Pathos, and Ethos are the three modes of persuasion defined by Aristotle to influence an audience effectively.

Logos (Logic & Reasoning): Appeals to logic and facts, using data, statistics, and logical arguments. Example: A climate activist cites scientific research to prove global warming.

Pathos (Emotions & Feelings): Appeals to emotions by using personal stories, imagery, or emotional language. Example: A charity ad showing a hungry child to evoke sympathy and encourage donations.

Ethos (Credibility & Authority): Establishes trust and credibility through expertise, ethics, or reputation. Example: A doctor endorsing a medical treatment, leveraging their professional credibility.

---

22. Aristotle and Robert Bartlett, *Aristotle's Art of Rhetoric* (Chicago, Chicago University Press, 2021), 12-72.

Canons of Rhetoric

| Figure 3.1 | Canons of Rhetoric |

The Five Canons of Rhetoric

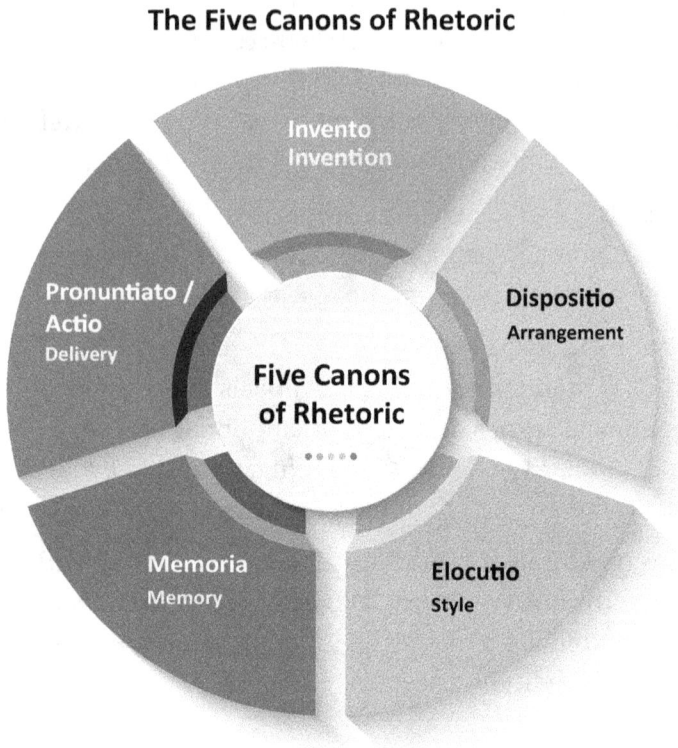

(Adapted from Patty Mulder, 2025)[23]

There are five canons of rhetoric, considered to be the five essential phases for developing a coherent and persuasive speech. It is generally believed that these canons were first codified in Rome by Cicero (the Roman orator) during the Classical Era or Period, and they consist of the following elements:

---

23. "Five Canons of Rhetoric (Aristotle)", Patty Mulder, accessed 15 Dcember, 2024, https://www.toolshero.com/communication-methods/five-canons-of-rhetoric/

Inventio (Invention): This refers to the process of developing impactful arguments by discovering the most effective ways to persuade an audience using the most appropriate arguments and evidence to support one's topic/theme.

Dispositio (Arrangement): This involves arranging or organizing one's speech properly, having an introduction, a body (that contains the main points), and a conclusion.

Elocutio (Style): This refers to the practice of selecting the most appropriate words and sentence structures in order to deliver an effective message to your audience. It involves utilizing rhetorical devices like alliteration, metaphors, and similes to improve the persuasiveness of one's speech.

Memoria (Memory): This canon, as far as classical rhetoric was concerned, focuses primarily on the practice of memorizing speeches. This may also mean having a firm grasp of one's speech material so as not to heavily depend on notes or a teleprompter to deliver one's speeches well.

Pronuntiatio (Delivery): As its name implies, this refers to the actual presentation of your speech. It may involve utilizing certain attributes for efficient delivery, including gestures, body language, tone of one's voice, and facial expressions.

In essence, the five canons should be considered as a comprehensive guide to help speakers craft and deliver speeches effectively.

3.2 Gathering Reliable Information

If I could divide speech-making into two procedures, the first and most important step is gathering the most appropriate information for your speech.

Figure 3.2 Sources of gathering information

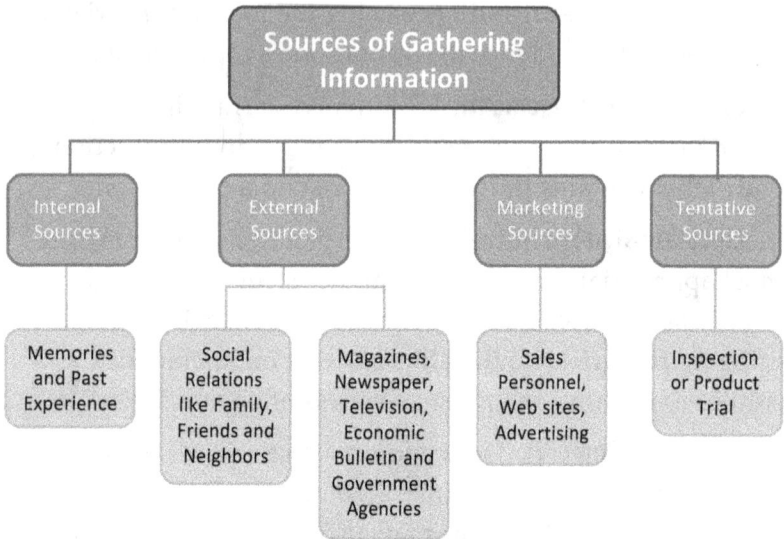

(Adapted from Mahmoud Ahmed Aboushouk , 2019)[24]

The second is delivering your speech. However, it doesn't matter how eloquent and confident you may be; if your message is poorly researched and organized, you are preparing yourself to become a failed speaker.

If your audiences aren't motivated and better informed by your speeches, chances are that you won't receive a second invitation to speak to them.

If you are wondering what the best approaches are for gathering useful information for your speeches, here are some of my helpful suggestions:

1. **Start early:** It is unprofessional to wait until the last few days or the last minute for your speech before researching what you are going to deliver to your

---

24. "Sources of gathering information", Mahmoud Ahmed Aboushouk, accessed 5 May, 2025, https://www.researchgate.net/figure/Sources-of-gathering-information_fig6_345814342

audience. Make it a habit to begin working on your research as soon as possible. This will give you enough time to find the right information and, if necessary, verify and refine it before the day of your speech.

2. **Ask yourself some critical questions:** To guide your information-gathering process, you may need to ask yourself some key questions, such as, What is the goal of the speech? Who is the audience? What kind of message will the audience (ask open-ended questions) find important and useful?

3. **Create a realistic research plan:** Take time to outline what information you are exactly looking for and list the possible sources for it. Give your research a timeline, explaining what should be accomplished within certain periods of time. If you are a very busy speaker, chances are that you are always on the road. You may not necessarily have adequate time to do a lot of research for each speech; hence, timing yourself while conducting informational research may help you to judiciously utilize your spare time.

4. **Identify key sources for your content research:** It is helpful to utilize popular sources such as reputable websites, books, encyclopedias, online libraries, and now text-generated artificial intelligence systems like ChatGPT, Gemini, and Copilot. You can equally use library databases, magazines, and academic journals. It is your responsibility to assess the credibility of your sources. For articles, pay attention to the author's credentials, the articles' publication dates, and their reputation.

5. **Conduct your preliminary research:** In this age of information overload, despite the large amount of information on the internet, speakers naturally struggle with making quick decisions about which

essential materials to include in their speeches. It is understandable that having access to a wide range of data or information on the same topic can be quite intimidating and confusing. The best thing to do is to start with a broad search to get an overview of your topic. From there, narrow down your speech's key points, since you won't have time to touch on all the broad points you have already discovered in the course of your research.

6. **Always take notes:** As you spend hours gathering your speech information, do not rely on your memory; always jot down some notes. You can organize them by themes, relevance, or main points. This will help you organize your speech logically.

7. **Collect some supporting materials:** In addition to gathering the main content for your speech, it is beneficial to collect supporting materials such as quotes, anecdotes, statistics, and relevant examples. These elements help reinforce your key points, add depth, and enhance the overall impact of your speech. Incorporating well-chosen supporting materials can make your message more engaging and compelling for your audience.

8. **Personal stories:** Reflect on your own life experiences for authenticity. You can gain some ideas from your own past actions and interactions with others.

9. **Current events/news:** Use trending topics to make your speech timely. Watching TV or listening to the radio can give you an idea of what is trending. People tend to respond actively to trending themes, especially some of the latest gists or memes on social media.

10. **Books & articles:** Read books, articles, and other periodicals to learn about recent quotes or stories from thought leaders.

11. **TED Talks/YouTube:** For inspiration on delivery and structure, watch several TED Talks and other helpful YouTube videos. You can learn a lot about how professional speakers start, moderate, and conclude their powerful speeches.

12. **Journaling:** Free-write to explore speech-worthy topics. Journaling can ignite your memory and bring some useful speech ideas back to your mind.

13. **Use AI for refining:** After gathering your speech ideas from diverse sources, you may need to refine them into powerful points. AI can be a useful tool for refining your speechwriting.

3.3 Organizing Your Research

Pat yourself on the back if you have successfully collected useful information from different applicable sources that you can use in your speech. The next important step is to properly organize your materials. Logically arranging your research materials has its own intrinsic benefit; it can help you prepare a coherent and impactful speech, from beginning to end.

Here are some necessary procedures a public speaker can follow while organizing their research:

1. **Identify your speech purpose and audience:** What is my speech all about? Who will I be speaking to? These two questions will assist you in identifying your speech's fundamental purpose and its audience. As soon as you are clear on these two interconnected elements— the purpose of your speech and the nature of your

audience—you will be able to select the best materials or content that will resonate strongly with them.

2. **Organize your notes:** After taking several notes, you are likely going to end up with a bunch of notes (handwritten or typed). You may choose to arrange your notes according to their topics, themes, or main points. Structuring your notes in this manner will streamline your speech writing.

3. **Develop an outline:** You should work on creating a detailed outline for each of your speeches. Your speech should have an introduction, body, and conclusion. Under each section, clearly arrange the necessary main points and their supporting evidence just as you are going to deliver them in front of your audience.

4. **Write a thesis statement:** Writing a full speech from scratch can be quite intimidating or overwhelming. It is advisable that you first develop a clear thesis statement that summarizes all the main points in your message. Without a doubt, this will help you organize the content of your speech appropriately.

5. **Choose your desired organizational pattern:** You may select an organizational pattern that perfectly suits your speech. Examples of popularly used organizational patterns include cause-effect, topical, chronological, problem-solution, and spatial.

   A. **Cause-effect organization:** In this case, speeches are arranged in a way that the causes of certain situations are directly connected to their effects. For example, a speaker delivering a speech on poor sleeping habits (effect) among young people can link that sleeplessness to their addiction to social media (cause).

B. **Chronological organization:** This is a speech pattern that demonstrates how the different pieces in a story or an event happen one after the other, in a timed sequence.

C. **Spatial speech pattern:** This speech style organizes information by how it perfectly fits together in a physical space.

6. **Incorporate some supporting materials:** One strategic approach through which speakers can spruce up their speech and make it appear more credible and reliable is by incorporating some supporting materials in them. These could be statistics, anecdotes, related examples, quotes, and so on. The supporting materials are basically used to buttress the main points raised in your speech. When adopted appropriately, they can improve the delivery of your speech by making it more engaging, interesting, and persuasive.

7. **Review and revise:** It is advisable that you review and update your speech outline and notes as many times as possible. You want to ensure that your gathered information flows in a logical manner and all important points are properly organized and well-supported. By taking these essential steps, as a public speaker, you will be able to deliver a clear, well-coordinated, and powerful speech.

3.4 Inform, Persuade, and Motivate (IPM of speech)

Every time public speakers appear in front of audiences, they potentially have three fundamental goals to achieve: to inform, persuade, and motivate their audiences. It is a fact that each of these three objectives requires a specific technique or strategy.

3.4.1. Inform

If your intention as a speaker is to pass some cogent information, new concepts, or insights to your audience, it is important to present your facts in a very clear and relatable way. Your audience's interest or engagement with your content will depend on how many interesting ideas they can derive from your speech.

More importantly, you should endeavor to structure your content rationally, starting with an introduction, body, and conclusion. If you are going to employ some supplementary content, such as statistics, quotes, anecdotes, etc., to support your points, make sure they are from credible sources. Do your best to keep your audience engaged by serving them relevant visuals, examples, and stories.

3.4.2 Persuade

As a public speaker, you can persuade your audience to embrace certain viewpoints or carry out a particular action. To accomplish this, you can adopt Aristotle's three persuasive appeal strategies that are explained below:

1. **Ethos:** As a speaker, you need to show that you are credible and have the necessary expertise in the topic you are delivering a message about. Your audience will listen attentively to you when they know that you are dependable based on your level of experience in the topic or subject matter.

2. **Pathos:** Consciously appeal to your audience's emotions by regaling them with passionate delivery, anecdotes, and understandable language.

3. **Logos:** Utilize vivid reasoning, concrete evidence, and logical arguments to support every claim you make in your speech. You may need to use counterarguments to

handle or oppose any opposition to the claims in your speech.

3.4.3. Motivate

Motivational speakers aim to encourage and stimulate their audiences to carry out a specific action or transform their worldview or behaviors. Explained below are some helpful strategies that can be applied in motivational speaking:

1. **Vision:** For your audience to take the exact action you are commending to them, you first of all need to show the benefits of doing so by painting a satisfying picture of the future for them.

2. **Passion:** Sometimes, audiences won't be convinced enough by the speakers' words, but they are more likely to be energized by the speakers' enthusiasm and assurance about the messages they are delivering.

3. **Call to Action:** Move your audience into action by giving them a clear and understandable call to action. Inform your audience about the possible benefits of doing so and, if possible, tell them convincing stories of people who had done so in the past and the benefits they derived from taking such an action.

4. **Personal Connection:** The most effective way to motivate your audience is to tell them some personal stories. By sharing some of your unique experiences with them, you can create a genuine bond between you and your audience.

Chapter Summary

- Logic, as defined by Aristotle, is a logic of argument employed to persuasively communicate with an audience. Having its inception in Classical Rome, there are five intrinsic cannons of logic, namely invention, arrangement, style, memory, and delivery. The five cannons of logic are considered to be very useful guides for public speakers.

- To write and present cohesive and highly effective speeches, public speakers have to gather crucial information or materials for their speeches from reliable sources such as credible websites, libraries, bibliographies, books, magazines, journal articles, etc.

- Once those materials have been successfully collected, it is imperative for speakers to arrange the information in their order of importance or relevance to their speeches' themes/ topics.

- In principle, speakers' primary responsibilities are to inform, persuade, and motivate their audiences.

Quiz

1. Who defined logic as *"a combination of the science of logic and of the ethical branch of politics"*?

   a. Cicero
   b. Aristotle
   c. Socrates

2. The five canons of logic were first codified during the classical era in _____ .

   a. Madrid
   b. Rome
   c. Athens

3. When it was first invented, the Greek philosophers limited the application of rhetoric to only civic and _____ uses.

   a. Scientific
   b. Historical
   c. Political

4. To motivate your audience as a speaker, you need to do all the following except _____

   a. Giving them a call-to-action
   b. Selling to them
   c. Establishing a personal connection with them

5. Motivational speakers primarily encourage their audiences to _____ .

   a. Buy a product or subscribe to a service
   b. Transform their behaviors and worldview
   c. Pay less fees for conferences/events

6. According to Aristotle, there are _____ persuasive appeals that a public speaker can adopt.

   a. Two
   b. Five
   c. Three

7. As a persuasive appeal strategy, "ethos" indicates a speaker's _____ .

   a. Emotional influence
   b. Credibility
   c. Logic

8. When speakers utilize concrete evidence and logical arguments to prove a point to their audience, this persuasive tactic is usually referred to as _____ .

   a. Ethos
   b. Logos
   c. Pathos

9. Namba, Inc. is a software company that has 2000 employees. Every year, it conducts an upskilling conference for its employees, inviting an experienced speaker to help introduce them to a new, useful skill. This year, they have invited Mr. Bill, a public speaker, to help them train their employees on "how effective communication among employees can improve their productivity". Mr. Bill, in this case, was hired to do what kind of public speaking?

   a. To inform Namba, Inc.'s employees about the benefits of effective communication skills
   b. To persuade the employees to be responsible in their workplace
   c. To motivate the employees to be good workers

10. Speakers don't necessarily need to undertake any research for their speeches.

    a. True
    b. False

Answer Key

1 – b	2 – b	3 – c	4 – b	5 – b
6 – b	7 – b	8 – b	9 – a	10 – b

CHAPTER 4

Structuring Your Speech

Key Learning Objectives

- Explore how to create a speech outline
- Understand the balance between main points and supporting details
- Learn how to time your speech

Writing an engaging and impactful speech will require you to follow certain routines every time you are preparing for a speech. In this chapter, I want to show you the strategies I usually employ to create most of my powerful speeches. I break them down into simple, doable processes that anyone can replicate, even if you didn't like writing as a student or when you were young.

To assist you, I will explain the significance of having an outline for your speech. I will also demonstrate how you can balance your speech's main points with some supporting details. One thing most speakers struggle with is timing; in this chapter, you will discover some useful techniques for time management.

4.1 Creating your Speech Outline

The outline mentioned in Chapter 3 was for organizing the materials obtained from your preliminary research. Here, I will be explaining how to create an effective outline to aid you in your speechwriting. If you want to maintain coherence and flow in your speech, you will definitely need a well-thought-out outline.

Let me show you how I craft my speech outline step by step!

Figure 4.1   **Speech Outline**

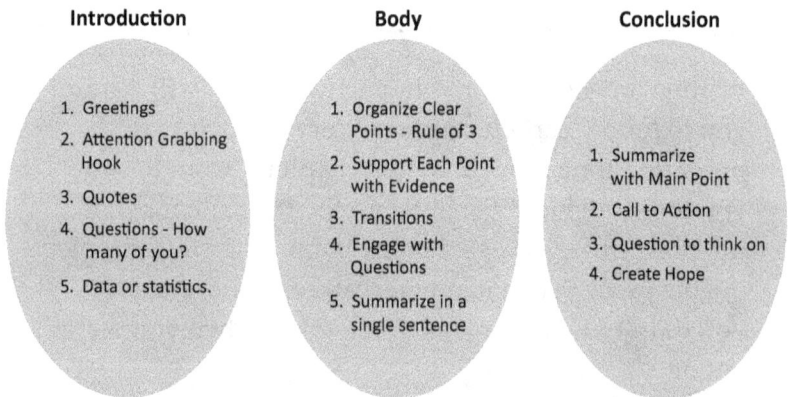

Introduction

1. Greetings
2. Attention Grabbing Hook
3. Quotes
4. Questions - How many of you?
5. Data or statistics.

Body

1. Organize Clear Points - Rule of 3
2. Support Each Point with Evidence
3. Transitions
4. Engage with Questions
5. Summarize in a single sentence

Conclusion

1. Summarize with Main Point
2. Call to Action
3. Question to think on
4. Create Hope

My entire speech is usually divided into three sections—introduction, body, and conclusion. Each of the sections contains vital elements.

4.1.1 Introduction

This contains my salutations or greetings. I usually begin my speech with a warm and respectful greeting to my audience. Over time, I have learned to greet my audience in their own language or jargon they are all familiar with. Sometimes, I start with *Hello, Good Morning,* or a simple greeting with high energy. I always make sure that whatever greeting I choose is acceptable to each member of my audience.

I also include an attention-grabbing hook line before I begin delivering my speech. Sometimes, I utilize a hook to pump my audience's excitement. This may be an interesting quote, a personal story, or relevant data or statistics. I usually start my speech with "How many of you…?" which is a great hook to connect with the audience at the beginning of the speech. For example, how many of you believe in the power of gratitude? Or how many of you have stage fright?

Another way for me to start my speech is by adding a quote. For example, if the speech is on "5 AM Club," I would start with "Early to bed, early to rise, makes a man healthy, wealthy, and wise."

In order to ensure that my introduction is apt and powerful, I will revise it repeatedly. Your introductions and endings are like an airplane taking off and landing — that's the time when maximum accidents happen. If your introduction is bland and uninteresting, your audience will think they have signed up for a boring speech.

4.1.2 Body

To produce a memorable presentation to my audience, I usually state my key points, highlight the subpoints, which are the supporting facts, proof, examples, tales, and so on, and then loop both the main points and subpoints together.

The body is where your message really comes to life.

Here's how to structure it effectively:

1. Organize with Clear Points

- Use the rule of three and decide on three key points to keep your speech focused and impactful.
- Order them logically. For example, if you're explaining a process, follow the steps chronologically.

2. Support Each Point with Evidence

- Use stories, examples, statistics, or quotes for each point to make it relatable and memorable.
- Don't overwhelm—one or two strong examples per point is usually enough.

3. Create Transitions

- Use transitions to flow smoothly from one point to the next. This keeps your audience on track.
- Phrases like "On the other hand…," "Let's move on to…," or "Another aspect to consider…" work well to link ideas.

4. Engage with Questions or Interaction

- Rhetorical questions or direct interaction, like asking for a show of hands, draws your audience in and keeps their attention on you.

5. Summarize Each Point Briefly

- After explaining a point, summarize it in a single sentence to reinforce your message and help your audience remember it.

Here are a few examples to help you understand better!

Example 1: The Importance of Time Management

1. **Identify Priorities**

    - **Example:** "A student balancing school and work stays focused by prioritizing tasks. Studies show that clear priorities reduce stress and boost productivity."

2. **Use Tools and Techniques**

    - **Example:** "Using the Pomodoro Technique – 25-minute focused work with short breaks – helps maintain energy and avoid burnout. A friend of mine used it in college and saw big improvements."

3. **Build Self-Discipline**

    - **Example:** "Self-discipline is like a muscle. A runner trains for a marathon by slowly increasing distance, just like setting small goals builds focus over time."

> ### Example 2: The Power of Positive Thinking
>
> 1. **Boosts Mental Health**
>   - **Example:** "Starting the day with gratitude reduces stress. People who focus on positives often feel more resilient and open to solutions."
> 2. **Improves Physical Health**
>   - **Example:** "Positive thinkers tend to have lower blood pressure. A doctor once shared how a hopeful patient recovered faster due to an optimistic mindset."
> 3. **Strengthens Relationships**
>   - **Example:** "Positive people are better communicators and listeners. A friend who always looks for the good tends to build deeper, more supportive connections."

4.1.3. Conclusion

Just like I mentioned at the beginning, it is crucial to summarize with the appropriate message at the end of every speech. I always conclude by summarizing some important points in the speech. For example, talking about teenage social media, I could conclude by saying that excessive use of social media by our teenagers has both negative and positive consequences. However, parents, teachers, and the government can collaborate to make social media safe and helpful to our teenagers' personal and academic development.

More often than not, I would restate my thesis statements before issuing my closing statement. To end my speech in a remarkable manner, I could use a call to action or present a promising hope to parents, teachers, and the government if all my main points and subpoints are properly considered.

4.1.4 Tips for writing a great speech outline

If you aspire to create a great outline for writing your speech, I will encourage you to pay attention to the following essential points:

1. **Be specific:** It is advisable that you draw up a specific outline that exactly fits your speech purpose, whether it is an informative, demonstrative, persuasive, or ceremonial speech. In short, your speech objectives will dictate what kind of content you should incorporate into it.

2. **Transitions:** No one delivers a speech in one straight flow; there will be some pauses and silences. Therefore, you need to create an outline that takes this fact into consideration. Your transitions should help you connect points smoothly without experiencing an awkward disruption in your delivery.

3. **Focus on the main points:** Let your speech writing focus primarily on the main points. In other words, due to time constraints in delivering your speech, there might not be time to digress into issues that are practically not for your speech purpose.[25]

---

25. Simon Lancaster, *Speechwriting: The Expert Guide* (The Crowood Press, 2010), 56-75.

4. **Review and rewrite:** No one promises that your first attempt to produce a speech outline will be perfect. It is important to review, rewrite, and update its content. This also explains why you should begin working on your speech several weeks or even months before it is scheduled for delivery.

4.2 Balancing Main Points and Supporting Details

If you want your speech to be clear, understandable, and memorable, it is imperative that you establish a balance between the main points and the supporting details used to advance the purpose of your speech. Personally, I have some strategies I have been employing over the years, and I am quite excited about discussing them with you below:

1. **Identifying my main points:** My first action is to identify the main points for my speech. The question you may want to ask may be, How do you know what should be the main or supporting points? In a situation where you have done a lot of research and are wondering what should count as your main points, I have the following golden nuggets to offer you:

    A. *Your main points are directly related to the topic given to you to prepare a speech on.*

    B. *Your main points are meant to address your audience's pain points.*

    C. *Depending on the purpose of your speech, your main points should inform, entertain, and persuade your audience.*

    As an experienced corporate trainer and public speaker, while working on the main points to include in my speeches, I often highlight the major issues or problems my audience wants some solutions to. I usually limit my main points to about 2–4, depending on the expected length of the speech. This helps me to be focused on the goals of my speech. In principle, my main points are usually included in my thesis statements, being the things my audience is yearning for.

2. **My supporting details:** I utilize a number of elements, data, or information to strongly support my main points. From using personal anecdotes and experiences to adopting examples, quotes, and statistics from others, my hope is to make my speech relevant to my audience. The supporting details provide the much-needed reinforcement for my main points and make it easier for my audience to enjoy my speeches. If you are not carrying your audience along as a speaker, something may be wrong with the quality and usefulness of your supporting materials.

3. **Structuring my speech:** It is not enough to have good main and supporting points; you must be able to smoothly combine them to create a coherent and well-articulated speech. I usually do this when structuring my speeches:

   A. *Choose the main point that tackles one of my audience's requirements or pain points.*

   B. *Incorporate a supporting detail—which can be a quote, a personal story, other people's ideas, statistics, etc.*

   C. *Summarize that thesis statement by summarizing both my main and supporting points.*

4. **Using transitions to create a balance:** Transitions are very useful elements, whether you are planning, writing, or delivering your speech. So, use them wisely. There

are two unique transitions I normally adopt when balancing my main points and their supporting details:

A. **Smooth Transitions:** Examples of my smooth transitions are phrases I normally use to connect my main ideas to my supporting points. They include phrases such as, *"Isn't it wonderful that…?" "Are you with me?" "Let's dive in further." "You will like this one!"* In fact, I have a list of over 200 smooth transitions in my file. You can create your own list of smooth transitions, too.

B. **Signposting:** Signposting, in speech, are expressions or phrases speakers use to create excitement in their audiences by letting them know that they are carrying them along from one main point to another. Some of my signposting phrases are *"first, second," "First step, second step." "My suggestion number 1, my suggestion number 2…".*

5. **Refining and updating:** Nothing gets done perfectly on the very first attempt; that is why I usually revise, refine, and update both my main and supporting points. I often advise my mentees, who are also great speakers, to rehearse their speeches' ideas or points aloud so that they can easily detect any inconsistencies in the messages they are passing across to their audiences. You can do the same by asking your colleagues who are speakers to offer some constructive criticism of your speech's main and supporting ideas in order to prepare a well-balanced speech.

4.3 Timing Your Speech

Speakers often struggle with managing their time effectively, especially when delivering their speeches.

Personally, I am grappling with the same situation. Every time I am on the stage, I want to make sure I keep my audience engaged by touching on all the key points in my speech. Unfortunately, in reality, this is very difficult to do because time flies when you are on stage. Before you can blink your eyes, you will probably have run out of your allotted time.

These are some of the strategies I am using to successfully manage my time as a speaker:

1. **Understanding that my time is limited:** Getting the right time is a matter of planning and practice. I have been learning to be mindful of every speech I do, from presentations to training programs, or keynote speeches, by planning and practicing again and again. If your practice is right, timings will go right.

2. **Simplifying my message:** One way to save time is to simplify the message. Not including too much, albeit unnecessary, helps me stay on what is relevant and useful for my audiences. One thing I would recommend to aspiring speakers is to embrace brevity in their speeches. By keeping their messages concise and brief, speakers can go straight to the point and successfully maintain their audience's interest in the messages being delivered.

3. **Planning my time:** The planning phase involves breaking down your talk into its main components — identifying each different idea or section and estimating how long each part will take. This is called a time budget because, well, time is limited, and you need to budget it just like you need to budget your money!

4. **Monitoring my speed:** I often monitor my time to gauge my speaking speed. If I am delivering a difficult speech, I normally adjust my pace so that my audience

can clearly catch every single statement I make during its delivery. It is not advisable for speakers to speak very fast. I think the most sensible practice is to maintain a moderate pace so that your audience can comprehend your message. In the case of presentation guidelines during training programs, I always leave at least 25% of my allotted time for Q&A, a minimum of two minutes (but usually closer to five) for my intro, and a couple of minutes for my conclusion. Once I have those off, I distribute the remaining time between each segment, estimating how long each segment will take. One segment might need four minutes, while another only gets 90 seconds.

5. **Practicing my speech:** By practicing your speech, whether in your bedroom while standing in front of the mirror or elsewhere, you can identify some sections of the speech that may warrant cutting. You should use a timer to record your average speech-delivery time. If you notice that you are spending most of your speaking time in sections that seem unnecessary, you can decide to remove those sections from your speech to check to see if you're on, under, or over time. If you're going over time, then you can either edit down that segment, get rid of the segment altogether, or steal time from elsewhere by editing or chopping out a different segment and redistributing the leftover time.

6. **Using pauses effectively in my speeches:** Pauses make it possible for me to properly manage the pace of my speeches. While I am silent for the briefest moments, it gives my audiences the chance to absorb and interact with my messages. As a result of this, I don't have to rush through my speech and allow my audience to internalize the message.

7. **Utilizing visuals wisely:** We all know that visuals or slides are great tools for conveying certain information to the audience. However, I abstain from using them a lot so as not to distract my audience. Moreover, I usually allocate time for each visual per speech to prevent overdependence on it.

8. **Engaging with my audience:** After all these years, I can confidently conclude that when your audience is feeling energized, they will naturally become interactive with you. This makes speeches go smoothly, and you can overcome the issue of lacking enough time to conclude, once your audience has already been captivated by what you have delivered to them.

Chapter Summary

- Preparing or writing a new speech from scratch can be quite intimidating. This is why it is usually advisable to create a useful outline containing all the necessary parts or sections that your speech will contain.

- To simplify the process of writing your speech, you should also divide the topic into both the main and supporting points.

- The main points are, by default, the main titles in your speech, while the supporting points are the subtitles or additional information used to expand the scope of or support your main points.

- Whether you are writing a speech or practicing it before delivery, everything can go very fast. It is advisable that you time your speech writing and rehearsing. By doing so, you will be able to discover how long it will take you to actually deliver each section of your speech on the stage.

Quiz

1. Any speaker who wants to present their ideas/content coherently and understandably must have _____ .
    a. a university degree
    b. an outline
    c. an attractive face

2. Which section in a speech should a speaker put "greetings"?
    a. Conclusion
    b. Introduction
    c. Body

3. Why is a speech's introduction very important?
    a. A good introduction can quickly catch the audience's attention
    b. Because it is usually the beginning of a speech
    c. Because all speakers must start with an introduction

4. Experienced public speakers will put their thesis statements in which section of their speeches?
    a. Conclusion
    b. Body
    c. Introduction

5. Which of the following is NOT one of the tips for writing an excellent speech outline?
    a. Being specific
    b. Using transitions
    c. Utilizing metaphors

6. Both in writing and delivering a speech, transitions can be used to create a balance between the main points and supporting points.

    a. True
    b. False

7. Signposting is an example of the _____

    a. Main point in a speech
    b. Transitions
    c. Supporting point

8. What is the best approach for structuring an effective speech?

    a. The main point is followed by the supporting points
    b. The supporting points come before their main point

9. Identify the main point and the supporting point in the following example.

    A: The causes of diabetes among the elderly

    B: Diabetes in the elderly could be caused by the excessive consumption of alcohol and processed foods.

    a. A is the supporting point
    b. B is the supporting point
    c. A is the main point

10. **Why is it helpful for public speakers to time their speech while rehearsing it?**

    a. The longer their speeches, the bigger their speaking fees

    b. To identify how long each section of their speeches will be

    c. To learn how they can speak faster to their audiences

Answer Key

1 – b	2 – b	3 – a	4 – b	5 – c
6 – a	7 – b	8 – a	9 – a	10 – b

CHAPTER 5

The Power of Storytelling

Key Learning Objectives

- Understand the importance of storytelling in every speech
- Learn what elements make up a good story
- Find out how you can weave in personal anecdotes and vivid language

Picture this—you're in an audience, expecting just another speech. The speaker begins with, "When I was seven, I stood on a bench to be heard in class..."

And suddenly, you're listening.

That's the power of storytelling.

Long before PowerPoint and podcasts, humans connected through stories. Today, in public speaking, storytelling still works wonders. It captures attention, builds emotion, and makes ideas unforgettable.

The best speakers don't just inform—they inspire. And stories are how they do it. Whether it's a personal moment, a clever analogy, or a powerful metaphor, stories help your message stick.

Before you learn to speak powerfully, learn to tell a powerful story.

5.1 Why Stories Matter

Every culture embraces storytelling as a tool or means of passing important messages or traditional information from the older generations to the younger ones. We can remember our grandparents' fables, how they had woven moral lessons into those educational and sometimes entertaining folklore.[26]

At schools, teachers regale their students with stories aimed at motivating them to perform at their best in their studies. By comparison, public speakers are not in any way different from our grandparents and teachers—all of them are making sincere efforts to simplify ideas, educate, and encourage us to grasp the important messages in their talk.

So, why do stories matter for public speakers? Well, from my experience as a public speaker and soft skills trainer, I outline below four major reasons I think stories matter a lot in public speaking:

---

26. Ty Bennett, *The Power of Storytelling: The Art of Influential Communication* (Verb Technology, Inc., 2013), 28-44.

Figure 5.1 Why do stories matter

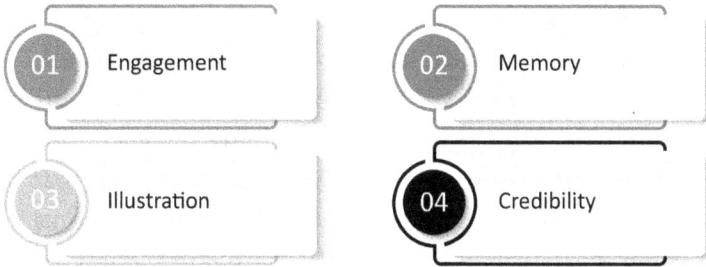

01 Engagement	02 Memory
03 Illustration	04 Credibility

1. **Engagement:** I have given speeches to various audiences, and I am confident when I say that storytelling does improve audience engagement. I have noticed on several occasions that stories captivate them, bring down the subject matter to their level, and make the ideas under discussion relatable to them. Speakers should understand that their audiences are comprised of human beings who dislike being confused and misled.

2. **Memory:** By default, most audiences remember interesting stories better than statistics and facts. This is because stories appeal to human emotions and logic. Most of us can still vividly remember some stories we were told when we were young, but not many of us can recall some lessons we were taught at school.

3. **Illustration:** Stories provide clear and memorable examples. The audience can, literally, picture in their minds whatever messages we are trying to convey to them if our stories are properly and creatively told. The messages will stick in their minds, and they will be able to bring them back from their memories several years later. One of the attributes of storytelling is that it is a great tool for entertaining the audience, and people tend to naturally remember things learned through comfort and enjoyment. As our stories linger in their

minds, they can use their own imaginations to create versions of them in their heads, thereby internalizing the core messages in the stories.

4. **Credibility:** The audience is open to stories that are believable, practical, and realistic. Speakers can build authority and credibility through the stories they tell. When advising new speakers, I often tell them that good stories can spark genuine discussions among their audience and can greatly motivate them to take some definite actions. Think of it this way—Stories are the essential oil we use to lubricate our speech-delivering engine. Without good, captivating stories, your audience will be left bored and unhappy.

5.2 Elements of a Good Story

Figure 5.2 Essential elements of a good story

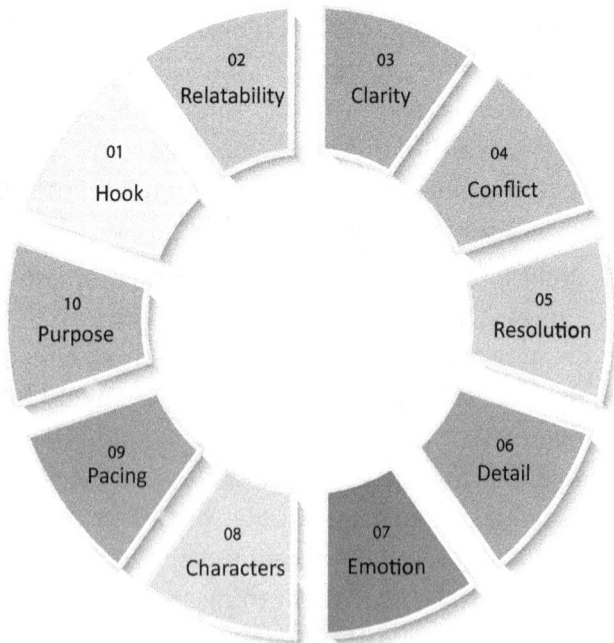

- 01 Hook
- 02 Relatability
- 03 Clarity
- 04 Conflict
- 05 Resolution
- 06 Detail
- 07 Emotion
- 08 Characters
- 09 Pacing
- 10 Purpose

Every good story consists of some fundamental elements or parts described below:

1. **Hook:** This is a story element used to grab the audience's attention immediately as the speaker begins to talk to them. A hook can be a quote, a surprising question, a statistic, or an image that quickly invites the audience into the speech. As a speaker, you have done a great job if you can successfully grab your audience's attention right from the beginning of your speech!

   Examples of Hook:

   A. **Quote:** *"The greatest glory in living lies not in never falling, but in rising every time we fall."* – Nelson Mandela

   B. **Surprising Question:** *"What if I told you that everything you've believed about communication is wrong?"*

   C. **Shocking Statistic:** *"Did you know that 93% of communication is nonverbal?"*

   D. **Powerful Image:** *Show a photo of a lone child sitting with a 'Will Speak for Food' sign to begin a speech on the power of public speaking.*

   E. **Short Story:** *"I was 8 years old, standing on a stage, hands trembling, and I forgot every single word of my poem. That moment changed my life..."*

2. **Relatability:** This answers these all-important questions: Can my audience relate to the story? Does it make any sense to them? Is the story connected to the audience's feelings and experiences?

3. **Clarity:** Your story must be clear and understandable to the target audience; otherwise, you are just wasting your precious time or jeopardizing your chance of carrying your audience along.

4. **Conflict:** There is, at least, one conflict in every story, which is the problem the story is all about. It is possible for a single story to address many issues or problems, but make sure the story doesn't appear confusing to your audience.

5. **Resolution:** This is the solution to the conflict or problem. The audience can heave a sigh of relief, having been told how the conflict was resolved.

6. **Detail:** A good story must be detail-oriented. In other words, it must offer vivid and appealing descriptions or explanations that the audience can relate to.

7. **Emotion:** The main reason speakers use stories is to elicit certain emotional reactions from their audience. A powerful story should be able to evoke strong feelings from the audience.

8. **Characters:** Naturally, stories are character-driven. It is usually effective for speakers to include some interesting characters that their audience can relate to.

9. **Pacing:** To carry your audience along, as a speaker, your story must have a good rhythm, and it should flow from the beginning to the end.

10. **Purpose:** Public speakers don't just use any story to drive a point. Instead, they select stories that are aligned with the themes of their speeches. At the end of their stories, they expect their audience to be mesmerized enough to the extent of responding quickly to a call to action.

5.3 Incorporating Personal Anecdotes, Metaphors, and Analogies

When coaching new speakers, I always emphasized the importance of utilizing the most appropriate stories to drive engagement and participation while delivering their speeches. This is to say that not all your stories will strongly resonate with your audience. You've got to be creatively selective.

In this section, I offer some cogent reasons while incorporating personal anecdotes, metaphors, and analogies, which can be a game-changing technique for you as a speaker.

Let's define the terms first:

1. **Personal anecdotes:** They are stories about you, your family, and other life experiences. They could be short or long stories, but it is usually advisable to make them short, sweet, and captivating.

2. **Analogies:** Analogies are a language element used primarily to compare one thing to another. For example, a speaker can say, "My childhood was as sweet as a bar of chocolate!" The speaker's audience can easily deduce that the speaker had a comfortable and happy childhood. Analogies can be employed to simplify a difficult topic or theme, using materials or ideas that the audience is quite familiar with. For example, practicing public speaking is like sowing a seed and watering it regularly. Consistent practice can make you an expert speaker.

3. **Metaphors:** A metaphor is a figure of speech that compares two dissimilar things and transfers the meaning of one to another. For example, we often hear people say, "Time is a thief." This can be translated into "Time is like a thief that steals some little moments of our life!"

I often incorporate personal anecdotes, analogies, and metaphors in my speeches for the following reasons:

- **Authenticity:** I want my speeches to be authentic, relatable, and memorable. Sometimes, our audience may struggle to remember everything we have told them at a conference or an event, but one thing they may not easily forget is the enchanting and genuine personal story we have regaled them with.

- **Engagement:** I have noticed on several occasions that whenever my audience was charmed by my great true-life stories, they tended to become more engaged in the event, laughing, asking questions, and offering their short opinions within the set timeframe.

- **Connection:** Sharing my personal experiences with my audience often establishes a strong connection between us. They seem appreciative of my dedication to them and their causes. Telling them my own private stories encourages them to see me as someone who is genuinely interested in helping them.

- **Inspiration:** I tell my personal stories to inspire and motivate my audience. Through empathy, I often encourage them to perceive themselves as capable and knowledgeable enough to succeed in whatever they set their minds to or lay their hands on.

- **Story Arc:** To be honest, storytelling gives speakers an opportunity to structure their speeches. A story arc begins with its introduction, progresses to the middle, and then comes to the climax (the story's end). A well-structured speech has about a 95% chance of fulfilling its purpose. Therefore, if used appropriately, storytelling helps speakers streamline their delivery, as they will not be short of material to include in their speeches.

- **Vulnerability:** When I tell a story about my personal experiences, I embrace my vulnerability to motivate my audience. I often show that I am a human being like them, and if I could succeed in my profession, they also stand a chance of becoming successful in theirs. When speaking to a diverse audience, storytelling is a unifying technique in the sense that we all share similar stories, irrespective of our cultures, ethnicities, levels of education, or financial status.

Chapter Summary

- Public speakers often utilize the art of storytelling to boost engagement with their audiences, demonstrate credibility, and clearly illustrate their core messages or ideas.

- The audience is likely to remember the interesting details rather than memorize every fact highlighted in the speech.

- Every good story has ten core elements—hook, relatability, character, conflict, resolution, clarity, emotion, detail, pacing, and purpose.

- When speakers incorporate personal anecdotes, metaphors, and analogies in their speeches, they are pushing for authenticity, improved engagement, and a deeper connection with their audiences.

Quiz

1. Utilizing storytelling is not important for a speaker aspiring to improve his/her engagement with the audience.

   a. True
   b. False

2. Which of the following is NOT the main reason why stories matter in public speaking?

   a. To encourage the audience to pay more.
   b. To increase audience engagement.
   c. To show how credible the speech ideas are.

3. Every great story must have a hook. What is referred to as a "hook"?

   a. A fascinating introduction.
   b. The middle of the story.
   c. The end of the story.

4. Which of these is NOT an element of an amazing story?

   a. The audience.
   b. Conflict.
   c. Character.

5. Why are speakers usually advised to "pace" their stories?

   a. Because their audience cannot understand the stories.
   b. They can add rhythm and flow to their stories.
   c. Because telling stories is not very important.

6. A figure of speech that compares two different things, transferring the meaning of one to the other is _____ .

   a. Hyperbole
   b. Oxymoron
   c. Metaphors

7. The expression "the girl is as kind as an angel" is an example of _____

   a. Interjection
   b. Oxymoron
   c. Simile

8. Which of the following BEST describes a "story arc"?

   a. Beginning, end, middle.
   b. End, beginning, middle.
   c. Beginning, middle, end.

9. Why do some speakers tell their own private or personal stories to their audience?

   a. For inspiration
   b. For boasting
   c. For deception

10. To appear genuine and reliable, some speakers show their own past mistakes and vulnerabilities to their audiences.

   a. True
   b. False

Answer Key

1 – b	2 – a	3 – a	4 – a	5 – b
6 – c	7 – c	8 – c	9 – a	10 – a

CHAPTER 6

Making Your Message Memorable

Key Learning Objectives

- Using visual aids effectively
- Incorporating statistics and facts
- Creating jaw-dropping moments

The modern audience has some preferences, and one of them is that they want to be served memorably when it comes to listening to speeches at an event, a seminar, or a conference. Public speakers, however, have risen to this challenge by utilizing a wide variety of visual aids, statistics, and facts in their speeches.

This chapter explores the practice of adopting the use of visual aids, facts, and statistics in speech delivery, highlighting their merits and possible demerits.

6.1 Using Visual Aids Effectively

It is estimated that about 65% of the population are visual learners, which indicates more than half of the population prefers acquiring new knowledge via visual aids. There are physiological factors contributing to the popularity of visual aids as speech-delivering or learning tools.

Figure 6.1 below explains how the human body responds to visual learning or visual aids.

Figure 6.1 **Some facts about visual learning**

1. Of all the information transmitted to the brain, 90% is visual

2. When compared to text, visual aids are processed 60,000 x faster.

3. Humans are capable of understanding visual aids in 1/10th of a second.

4. 40% of nerve fibres are connected to the retina.

5. Human brains can see images that last for only 13 milliseconds.

6. Human eyes can register 36,000 visual messages every hour.

(Source: Dana Jandhyala, eLearning Industry, 2024)[27]

27. Dana Jandhyala, "Visual Learning: 6 Reasons Why Visuals Are The Most Powerful Aspect Of eLearning," *eLearning Industry,* 25 October, 2024. https://elearningindustry.com/visual-learning-6-reasons-visuals-powerful-aspect-elearning

6.1.1 How to use visual aids effectively

There is a long list of visual aids that speakers can use for delivering their speeches. They include infographics, slide shows, posters, charts and graphs, whiteboards, videos, handouts, 3D models, physical props, demonstrations, etc.

In addition to having useful virtual aids, it is equally important to know how to effectively use them. I offer some practical pieces of advice below concerning how you, as a speaker, can drive the dynamics of your speeches with visual aids:

1. **To complement your message:** The best practice is to utilize your visual aids to enhance your points. It is not appropriate to allow your visuals to replace or overshadow your content or materials.

2. **To simplify your message:** Speakers may be tempted to cram a lot of information on their PowerPoint slides or infographics. This will only result in cluttering your visuals and muddying things up for your audience. To ensure that your audience can obtain as much information as they require, it is advisable to always keep your slides clean, concise, and straight to the point, with minimum text used.

3. **Make it relevant:** One mistake that can derail your speech delivery is the careless utilization of some visual aids that are not directly related to your core message. I don't think that your audience will overlook that error.

4. **Be professional:** After interacting with an audience on several occasions, one may become quite familiar with them. However, under no circumstances should you use any visual aids that are full of errors or reflect racist and sexist undertones. Your audience may be

pissed off by that, and they may find it difficult to overlook your unprofessional attitude.

5. **Clarity matters:** It is a fact that speakers have a lot to say within a short, allotted period of time. That doesn't give you the license to clutter your visual aids with many materials. You must ensure that your text is readable and the images on your slides aren't blurred or invisible. It is your responsibility to make your message clear and concise for your audience to understand.

6. **Be consistent:** It is important to utilize a uniform style for layouts, colors, and fonts while designing your visuals. Maintaining consistency can help reinforce your brand recognition because people who see your visuals can immediately identify them with your brand.

7. **Achieve a high level of engagement:** Visuals should be primarily used to capture the audience's attention and retain it for as long as possible. When I am training professionals, for example, I always incorporate facts, figures, and practical examples in my slide show so that they can absorb useful information required in their respective jobs or professions.

8. **Embrace variety:** I often experiment with a mixture of visuals that may include charts, videos, images, and my favorite being props. My goal is to keep my audience excited about my messages. When addressing a diverse audience, I also pay serious attention to the cultural sensitivity and professional requirements of each audience segment. I want to make sure everyone is being served properly and well. It may hurt your brand as a public speaker if half of your audience

cannot gain anything from your speech after spending nearly an hour listening to it.

FUN FACT

Japanese technique called Pecha Kucha

This unique format of the presentation involves using only 20 image slides, which are to be delivered in a total of 6 minutes and 40 seconds, allowing for 20 seconds per slide. This is a great example of how you can create an impact when visual aids are used to tell a riveting story (visual storytelling), talking less and showing more.

Advantages of Pecha Kucha: It helps speakers to properly prepare for their speeches. Moreover, they can stay within their assigned time slots or limits, and slides just have pictures and no text.

9. **Ensure that your visuals are accessible:** Some of your audiences may have people who are affected by color blindness or are visually impaired; it is your responsibility to ensure that your audience can clearly see and comprehend the messages displayed on your aids. Failure to do so may result in having dissatisfied sections of your audience who may not have gained anything during your entire speech. The best practices involve using readable font sizes, including captions and subtitles in your videos, using clear descriptions for your links, utilizing color contrasts to emphasize text importance, and using concise and understandable alt text to describe your images.

10. **Time your presentation:** Never be tempted to let your visuals replace your core messages while delivering

speeches. Instead, they are meant to reinforce your
ideas, but it is advisable that you use them sparingly.
On most occasions, what an audience is looking for
is a speaker who authoritatively uses his/her voice
while discussing a subject matter and creatively
connects his/her visuals to the core messages in order
to make himself/herself understandable to their
audience. However, time is limited; it is unproductive
to focus most of your speech-delivering time on
utilizing visuals. In this case, the visuals will become
distractions rather than being a useful reinforcement
for your core message. This entails that you should
appropriately time your presentation to avoid
allocating unduly long hours to utilizing visuals.

6.2 Incorporating Statistics and Facts

A dry speech, so to speak, lacks enthusiasm and fails
to connect with the audience on a deeper level. Without
incorporating relevant statistics and facts in your speeches,
they may become dry, boring, and not particularly useful to
your audience.

Speakers who embellish their speeches with statistics and
facts do command some respect from their audience. The
issue is not just about incorporating facts and statistics in
your speeches, but it is about doing so effectively.

Some of the best practices in the public speaking industry
are to include statistics and facts that meet the following
criteria:

1. **Relevance:** Use only relevant statistics and facts that
    will provide concrete support for the ideas or points in
    your speeches.

2. **Clarity:** Your statistics and facts, which are considered additional materials for presenting your messages, must be simple and direct for your audience to understand.

3. **Visualization:** Use your graphs and charts to visualize ideas. You can illustrate data with either numbers or text, or a combination of both, to help your audience grasp the core messages you are passing across to them.

4. **Context:** Always provide the necessary context that will help the audience understand the significance of your charts and statistics.

5. **Sources:** When preparing your charts or quoting some statistics, always use sources that are credible.

6. **Balance:** Maintaining balance in the use of statistics and charts can enhance your speech. In other words, you should avoid packing a large number of them in each of your speeches; otherwise, you will unintentionally overwhelm your audience.

7. **Storytelling:** Most experienced speakers weave engaging stories into their charts to make them appealing to their audience.

8. **Impact:** By utilizing surprising statistics, great speakers capture their audience's attention with the numbers depicting or explaining some facts in the statistics.

9. **Comparison:** The primary reason why experienced speakers compare their statistics with others is to highlight the differences and similarities between the facts represented on the charts or in the statistics.

10. **Practice:** Everything can be learned, including how to responsibly use statistics and charts in your speeches. More importantly, it is advisable that you practice, from time to time, how to properly do this so that

you can always deliver flawless presentations when incorporating statistics and charts.

6.3 Creating Jaw-Dropping Moments

While crafting your speeches, you should include content that will help you create jaw-dropping moments. These moments could invoke laughter, surprises, shocks, or even tears from your audience. It indicates that your messages, as a speaker, are emotionally connected with them.

The truth must be told: It is not every time that speakers can make their audience cry, laugh, or produce physical reactions to their speeches. You have to learn how to do this as you proceed in your career as a public speaker.

From my personal experiences, I provide some of the techniques below that have worked for me in creating memorable and jaw-dropping moments with my diverse audiences:

1. **Powerful Opening:** I started most of my memorable speeches with powerful and impactful stories, facts, questions, or quotes.

2. **Emotional Hooks:** After conducting a proper audience analysis and knowing who they are and what they are passionate about, I usually make serious efforts to connect emotionally with them by telling them what they are excited about hearing.

3. **Unexpected Twists:** When preparing my speeches, I usually insert some twists or turns or shocking subplots, such as using surprising facts or engaging personal stories. My goal is to increase my audience's excitement about my speeches.

4. **Pacing:** Experienced public speakers build excitement in their audiences gradually, up to the climactic levels by varying their speeches' pacing.

5. **Interactive Elements:** While writing my speeches, some of the interactive elements I usually employ include questions or activities that my audience members can work on together.

6. **Dramatic Pauses:** I don't just speak the whole time; I intentionally create moments of silence or pauses in my speech scripts to allow my audience to think creatively about the points or ideas in my speeches.

7. **Strong Conclusion:** I don't just begin my speeches with strong and unforgettable introductions; I equally end my speeches with calls to action or captivating statements.

Here's a template from my personal experience that has helped me create a jaw-dropping moment in my speech!

Template: 7 Powerful Elements of a Jaw-Dropping Speech

Case Study: J.K. Rowling's Harvard Commencement Speech[28]

1. Powerful Opening

Definition:
Start with a hook – a relatable story, surprising fact, quote, or question that grabs attention instantly.

---

28. J.K. Rowling and J.K. Rowling, "Text of J.K. Rowling'S Speech," Harvard Gazette, January 10, 2024, https://news.harvard.edu/gazette/story/2008/06/text-of-j-k-rowling-speech/.

Rowling's Example:
"I've lost weight from fear and nausea preparing this speech."

Reflective Question for Coaches:
What is one way you can open your next speech that instantly surprises or entertains your audience?

2. Emotional Hooks

Definition:
Connect with the audience's feelings and values by sharing personal vulnerability or a relatable emotion.

Rowling's Example:
"She openly shared her experience of poverty and loneliness as a single mother."

Reflective Question:
What personal story can you share that will emotionally connect with your audience's pain or dreams?

3. Unexpected Twists

Definition:
Introduce a surprise—turn failure into power, or share an insight that flips the audience's perspective.

Rowling's Example:
"Rock bottom became the solid foundation on which I rebuilt my life."

Reflective Question:
What's a life event that seemed like a failure but turned out to be a turning point?

4. Pacing

Definition:

Use speed variation in voice and delivery—slow down during emotional parts, speed up during energy moments.

Rowling's Example:

"Balanced slow reflective moments with energetic insights about empathy and imagination."

Reflective Exercise:

Practice a part of your speech using both slow and fast pacing. Notice the effect.

5. Interactive Elements

Definition:

Involve your audience—either with literal interaction or mentally engaging questions.

Rowling's Example:

Asked reflective questions like: "What's more dangerous—monsters or those who enable them?"

Reflective Question:

What question can you ask that makes your audience think or feel deeply?

6. Dramatic Pauses

Definition:

Use silence intentionally to let important messages land.

Rowling's Example:

"I had feared poverty, and I was still alive..." [Pause]

Practice Prompt:

Highlight one sentence in your speech where you will pause. Practice it now.

7. Strong Conclusion

Definition:

End with a call to action, a memorable quote, or a final thought that echoes in their minds.

Rowling's Example:

"We carry all the power we need inside ourselves already: we have the power to imagine better."

Reflective Question:

What is the one line you want your audience to remember after your speech?

Your Speech Planning Worksheet

Element	Your Version (Fill this)
Powerful Opening	
Emotional Hook	
Unexpected Twist	
Pacing Strategy	
Interactive Moment	
Dramatic Pause Point	
Strong Conclusion	

Chapter Summary

- Public speakers have many communication tools at their disposal that they can use to simplify and enhance their speech delivery. One of them is visual aids.

- However, it is important that speakers use their visual aids effectively to achieve their desired purposes.

- By incorporating statistics and facts in their speeches, public speakers can give well-balanced, clear, and relevant messages to their audiences.

- Some of the elements public speakers can incorporate in their speeches to create jaw-dropping moments include, but are not limited to, powerful openings, emotional hooks, dramatic twists, pacing, pauses, powerful conclusions, etc.

Quiz

1. Using statistics and charts in your speeches as a public
    speaker is a useless act.

    a. True
    b. False

2. Communication tools such as slide shows, posters,
    charts and graphs, whiteboards, and videos are
    collectively known as _____ .

    a. Infographics
    b. Visual aids
    c. Charts

3. It is believed that _____ of U.S. population are visual
    learners.

    a. 75%
    b. 65%
    c. 85%

4. Similarly, it is shown that out of all the information
    transmitted to human brains, _____ of it is visual.

    a. 70%
    b. 80%
    c. 90%

5. Which of the statements describes the worst approach
    for using visuals?

    a. Using it to cover all the messages.
    b. Using them for one-third of the speech-delivery
        time.
    c. Using them sparingly.

6. Two speakers use two different infographics for the same event. Speaker A's infographic is designed with illegible font sizes, while Speaker B's is created with readable font sizes and color contrasts to emphasize important texts. Which speaker has an infographic with an accessibility issue?

   a. Speaker A.
   b. Speaker B.

7. When a speaker attempts to rouse his/her audience's emotions at the beginning of his/her speech, this is a typical example of _____.

   a. Emotional hooks
   b. Pacing
   c. Captivating conclusions

8. When preparing their statistics and charts, speakers shouldn't worry whether their sources are credible or not.

   a. True
   b. False

9. It is possible for public speakers to use their graphs and charts to visualize ideas and thoughts while delivering their speeches to the audience.

   a. True
   b. False

10. **Why are speakers usually advised to maintain consistency in the design of their visual aids?**

    a. So that their audience can easily identify their brands.

    b. Because making new visual aids is very expensive.

    c. Because their audience doesn't like seeing new visual aids.

Answer Key

1 – b	2 – b	3 – b	4 – c	5 – a
6 – a	7 – a	8 – b	9 – a	10 – a

CHAPTER 7

The Art of Delivery

Key Learning Objectives

- Explore different methods of delivery
- Learn how to find your style
- Understand the importance of practicing for perfection
- Gain a better understanding of time management

Good speakers are remembered, but great speakers are repeated.

How many of you believe in this?

Well, this is the art of delivery.

Think about it—when Martin Luther King gave his speech, all you remembered was "I have a dream".

When Neil Armstrong landed on the moon, what line was etched in history? "One strong step for man, one giant leap for mankind."

We don't just remember these words—we repeat them. That's the impact of powerful sound bites, crafted intentionally through the art of delivery.

Your audience should be able to *repeat and recall* the essence of your talk without notes. That's your real takeaway.

In this chapter, we'll dive into the different modes of speech delivery and help you find your own unique style. And remember—practice is non-negotiable. It helps you become time-aware, confident, and clear on your delivery rhythm.

Let's explore how to make your message not just heard, but *echoed*.

7.1 Different Methods of Delivery

There are a few types of speech delivery techniques that public speakers employ. All approaches have their own advantages and drawbacks. The speech context, the target audience, and the speech objectives all influence the type of delivery style that should be used.[29] Let's explore the most common examples of speech delivery techniques.

---

29. Tim Polland, *Mastering the Moment: Perfecting the Skills and Processes of Exceptional Presentation Delivery* (Conder House Press, 2019) 45–66.

Figure 7.1 | Types of speeches

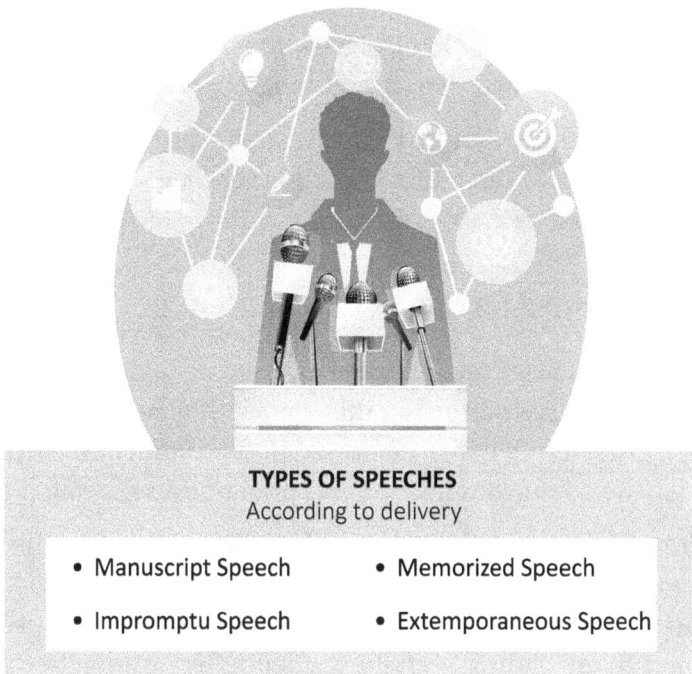

TYPES OF SPEECHES
According to delivery

- Manuscript Speech
- Memorized Speech
- Impromptu Speech
- Extemporaneous Speech

(Adapted from English with Ayesha, 2025.)[30]

7.1.1 Delivery of Manuscript

This is similar to a method called reading aloud verbatim. This is a technique you often see in formal contexts—say, a political speech or a trial where each word matters.

Pros: Having control over the terminology and precision in this manner is crucial for any high-stakes presentation you are trying to interject professionalism or authority into. It saves you from losing the score of that required point or idea.

---

30. "Types of Speeches",English with Ayesha, accessed 5 July, 2025, https://www.youtube.com/watch?app=desktop&v=lO0t4TWpkxk, YouTube, 19:19.

Cons: If intonation and direct eye contact are not applied, reading verbatim makes you sound like a robot. It also restricts the ability of a speaker to converse on the fly at an event. The speaker could also grow monotonous if they do not vary their speech, speed, and tone.

Context: This delivery style is utilized in almost every legal declaration, ceremonial and political speech, or in some situations that need exact wording.

7.1.2 Memorized Delivery

The speaker delivers a no-notes speech, memorized verbatim. The speaker using this approach must be capable of remembering (having memorized) the complete speech; that is why so much rehearsal and preparation are called for.

Pros: The primary advantage of memorized delivery is being able to maintain eye contact and interact with the audience more directly. This can increase the effect of speech and improve bonding with the audience. In addition to the speech being memorized, presenting information can be enhanced by powerful gestures and body movement.

Cons: Memorized delivery also brings with it various risks. A speaker could end up getting stuck staring off into space or even become frantic for leaving out that one key component. The more comfortable you are with your delivery, the less memorization pressure there is— this helps in making it sound more like a conversation rather than a script or foreign in tone.

Context: This type is best used when the speaker wants to come off as particularly polished or be brief and powerful with their words. For example, in theatrical productions or speech contests.

7.1.3 Impromptu Delivery

This refers to when you have not planned or written down what you will say in your speech. Impromptu delivery is the technique used in situations where a speaker is asked to respond on the spot (like when fielding an unexpected question).

Pros: The most significant takeaway from impromptu delivery is that it sounds natural and conversational, which works well for the speaker to present realistically. A regular practice of impromptu delivery is a great technique that can help you structure your thoughts well. Impromptu speeches are a great way to dare yourself to overcome stage fright.

Cons: On the downside, not having a plan might mean your message is all over the place, and you are thinking in chaos. Improvising (a skill that is challenging for those who are slow thinkers) or speaking off the cuff can land you knee-deep in filler words, vocal tics, and rambling territory.

Context: Impromptu delivery is often used for examples like Q&A sessions, interviews, or unscripted speaking engagements where authentic and off-the-cuff reactions are more important than presentation precision, such as self-introduction in group settings.

7.1.4 Extemporaneous Delivery

Extempore is like being told, "Your topic is X. You have 2 minutes to think." *Impromptu* is like being suddenly handed a mic and told, "Say something now!"

Both are excellent tools to train your spontaneity, structure, and confidence. And both can be practiced using frameworks like PREP (Point-Reason-Example-Point) or Past-Present-Future.

It's a structured approach that can be used in a variety of contexts, including:[31]

- **Impromptu speeches:** The PREP method can help reduce stress and help you think of what to say.

- **Writing:** The PREP method can help improve the structure and clarity of your writing.

- **Job interviews:** The PREP method can help you answer open-ended behavioral questions without rambling.

- **Meetings:** The PREP method can help you raise ideas clearly and succinctly.

Great speakers utilize the PREP method to professionally handle the pressure from being asked to deliver an impromptu speech. The PREP method entails:

- **Starting with the main point:** Begin with your main idea or recommendation.

- **Supporting the main point with reasons:** Provide logical justifications for your point.

- **Using relevant examples:** Reinforce your point with real-world examples or personal anecdotes.

- **Summarizing and/or concluding what has been said:** Reaffirm your point and conclude.

---

31. Kenneth, Acha. The PREP Framework: An Easy Way to Give Excellent Impromptu Speeches. *Servants University,* accessed 4 April, 2025, *https://www.servantsuniversity.com/the-prep-framework-an-easy-way-to-give-excellent-impromptu-speeches/*

> **Example:**
>
> **Point:** We should adopt a Hybrid Work Environment.
>
> **Reason:** It improves productivity and employee satisfaction.
>
> **Example:** Our Pilot program last quarter saw a 20% increase in output.
>
> **Point:** Therefore, we should improve the hybrid work environment.

Preparation and organization of content in advance, while speaking off-the-cuff (not tied to a script), is called extemporaneous delivery. It offers the speaker a way to tailor their message in real-time based on what is landing well and getting responses from your audience, keeping everyone active in an overall more casual style.

This type of speech delivery contains the pros of both worlds—it gives enough structure to deliver a well-organized speech, but also allows a change in delivery style based on audience feedback. Notes help the speaker stay on message without being completely dependent upon them, making for a more engaging and authentic delivery.

Pros: It gives enough structure to deliver a well-organized speech but allows an in-the-moment change in delivery style.

Cons: The flexibility of improvisational delivery is a strength, but it also means that there has to be a careful balance of planning and persistence, which can come off as a difficult thing to achieve. You can still rely on your notes, and if you do not practice sufficiently, it may come across as less refined than a memorized or manuscript speech.

Context: Improvised delivery is used in professional settings such as university lectures, conference talks, and business presentations whenever the speaker cannot just send a recording of his or her message.

7.2 Finding Your Style

Part of being an effective public speaker is developing a unique speaking style. Your style should match your personality, strengths, the context of your speech, and your audience's expectations. Having your own recognizable style will further showcase you as a professional speaker who has a special brand.

Follow these steps to find and develop your own unique speech delivery style:

1. **Self-Assessment**

   - **Assess Strengths and Weaknesses:** The foundation of your style comes from identifying what you are really good at while also pinpointing areas that need some work. Are you naturally funny, caring, or bossy? Perhaps it is storytelling you are good at, or great at simplifying complexity. Identifying these traits will allow you to use them more efficiently and create a successful but authentic style.

   - **Get Real:** Being authentic is key to developing trust with your audience. It is the way we naturally talk that makes people feel they can truly get to know us. It is not advisable to mimic the specific style of another speaker if it is not compatible with your personality. Instead, focus on building a unique voice that is your own.

2. Analysis of Audience

- **Audience Preferences:** Understanding the needs and wants of different audiences will allow you to adapt your speech delivery style quickly. Consider the context of your event, how much knowledge the audience already has about the subject matter, their interests, and their cultural backgrounds. A formal business conference will require a more authoritative and professional-sounding voice compared to, say, an informal community event where you would want it to sound friendly and casual.

- **Engage With Audience:** Public speaking means that you are conversing with the audience and not necessarily engaging in a monologue. Using rhetorical questions, anecdotes, and examples can make your speech more interesting and understandable to your audience.

3. Feedback and reflection

- **Accept constructive criticism:** Improve yourself by using the feedback you've got from others. Sometimes what people are saying may enhance your communication skills; they can be an outsider or a third person, peers, mentors, or speaking coaches who are experienced speakers themselves.

- **Look Back at Previous Performances:** If you are looking to gain insight into how to articulate a speaker you believe yourself to be, one way to do this is by watching your past presentations. Remember how you project yourself to the crowd in your tone, cadence, and body language. It will enable you to take a step back and see what happened with your presentation so that in the future, there is room for improvement.

4. **Continuous Improvement**

- **Try new things** — Public speaking is a muscle you have to work on, so don't give up on finding what works for you. Use these spoken topics, humor, stories, and rhetorical strategies in all of your speeches. See how your audience reacts and change it accordingly.

- **Figure out your method:** As you communicate in different scenarios and gain more experience, it is only natural that your style will change. Accept this change and be ready to adapt your strategy accordingly. In the end, improving your speaking abilities will always make you a better speaker and force you to be more confident as well.

TIP

One brilliant method that works for me is PAM, which stands for:

1. **P:** Phrases, try out new phrases.
2. **A:** Analogies, try new and different analogies.
3. **M:** Me, my story, my jokes, my life experiences to be shared.

We all have our own style of trying new things and building that public speaking muscle. You can build your own method.

7.3 Practicing for Perfection

The reality is that even those who seem to speak effortlessly have worked so hard (however, it may not feel like work if you love what you are doing or talking about) to be better public speakers. Even the most experienced and charismatic extroverted speakers know this to be true.

And, when you rehearse properly for your next presentation, it's not just about learning the words: rather, it's getting in touch with both the rhythm and pace of your performance. Such familiarity fosters self-assuredness, which lowers the probability of stuttering or struggling to find your words. In addition, practice helps you deliver exactly right: the way in which your voice, tone, and speed combine with how effectively it conveys what needs to be said.

Public speaking is a skill you can develop and hone, but it requires time. The more you do that, the better you will become over time because it helps with learning everything. Another benefit associated with doing this is that you will feel more comfortable, and therefore, you will have a performance that feels less rehearsed. This enables you to sound much more natural, intimate, and connected with your audience than fumbling over which line or explanation comes next.

Practice is just the bridge between knowing everything you need to know and walking out of your comfort zone in confidence with it all. It will transform your usual frightened start of public speaking into a confident and composed presentation in front of your audience. Practice leads to perfection, and perfection leads to success.

With that in mind, here are some of the ways you can work on practicing even more and grow your public speaking skills to elite status, where they will really shine during any presentation:

| Figure 7.2 | Effective delivery techniques |

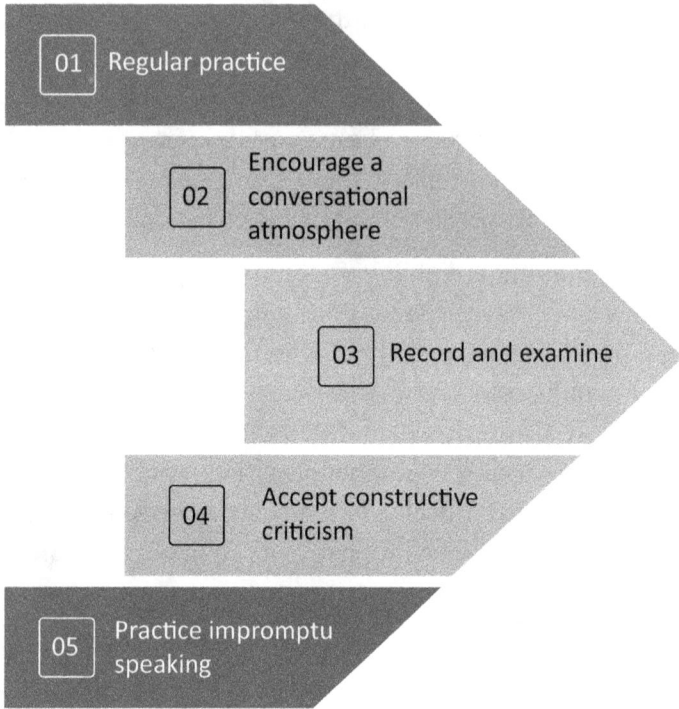

1. Regular Practice

- **Practice daily:** It builds memory muscle because it is the only way you will retain what you know. Treat practice as a part of your preparation and set aside specific time to work on your speeches. Consistency is key to using your voice with confidence and flow.

- **Close attention to important details:** Pay close attention to the essential components of your speeches throughout rehearsals, including body language, tone, tempo, and transitions. These components help create a dynamic and captivating delivery that keeps your audience interested and your point of view clear.

2. Encourage a conversational atmosphere

- **Engage in similar settings:** Nervousness-reducing and confidence-building practice can come from rehearsing in the same space that is similar to where you are actually going to speak. To this extent, you can practice in a room or space that is similar to your presentation venue.

- **Visual aids:** Practice those slides or other visuals used in your presentation to ensure seamless integration. One approach to minimizing the likelihood of technical difficulties during your conference is to rehearse with your visuals so that you will be more familiar with how they can be used better.

3. Record and examine

- **Video recording:** When you video record your practice sessions, it will allow you to gain valuable feedback and understand areas of improvement. Click, watch the video, and observe how you move, how you look, and your whole behavior. Make a list of where you need to improve by reducing some distracting habits or making your body language on point.

- **Audio recording:** Audio recordings of your practices can help you evaluate the delivery rate and identify spots where you need to improve on your tone, pacing, and timing. Be sure to add in things like vocal tics or filler words, how they are pitched (highs/lows), and how loud and clear they sound. Listening to audio recordings can help you judge your pacing and track how well your speech is structured.

4. **Accept constructive criticism**

- **Peer review:** You can always practice and then get your mentors or other trusted professionals to watch what you did. They can provide valuable feedback and suggest specific areas to focus on. Invite them to contribute ideas, but use them only to make the way you present it better.

- **Self-analysis:** Carry out a critical analysis of your practice sessions to get some insights about your speech delivery style. Figure out where exactly you are weak and start working on those weaker areas step by step. Set goals for every practice session and measure your progress over time.

5. **Practice impromptu speaking**

- **Sharpen your thinking on the spot:** Talking spontaneously all the time will make you an expert at dealing with any immediate situation and look absolutely incredible while doing it. When the audience asks a question, we end up repeating back the last thing they said—and that can be very useful when taking questions from the crowd or even just speaking off-the-cuff during your talk.

- **Get some prompts:** Come up with spontaneous topics for short speeches. It develops your C.R. (coherent and relevant way) of responding and would also help you in arranging your thoughts quickly, as well as their growth to their full potential.

7.4 Managing Time

If you wish to deliver an impressive speech, time management skills are crucial. Sticking to your 2–3 minutes means that you can ensure everyone will both hear and care about what you have to say. In this case, it also avoids halting the general schedule of an event and shows a certain amount of respect for their time. Here are ways you can manage your time skillfully in presenting a speech:

1. **Know Your Time Limit**

   - **Understand the time limits:** Write your speech keeping in mind that you do not have all the time in the world. Recognize your time limit so you do not have to hurry through and end up whiplashing or confusing your audience by putting too much information in their heads.

   - **Flexibility:** Give a little time to the interruptions or any in-between interactions with the audience. Flexibility may be required in relation to your scheduling, speech delivery, and crowd management during presentations.

2. **Plan and Structure Your Sections**

   - **Organize your speech:** Naturally, of course, your speech will be broken down into three parts, such as the introduction, body, and conclusion. Do your best to properly organize your speech to reflect these three components.

   - **Use time cues:** In your speech, plan visual or audio time cues for timeliness. For example, you could have a timer/watch nearby to keep an eye on. A noiseless alarm can vibrate to alert you that your allotted time for the presentation is coming to an end soon.

3. **Use a Timer to Practice:**

   - Always practice timing your rehearsals. This will prevent you from lingering on your speech parts longer than necessary. You can even build some flow when you ensure that every section of your speech has been adjusted for length.

- **Tweak as needed:** Sometimes your speech may go longer than expected; feel free to tweak it without changing its important components. Prepare to drop unnecessary segments from the speech or substitute them with different materials that are more important, so as to achieve balance in your presentation.

4. **Adapt on the Fly:**

- **Focus on the main ideas:** Determine the key components that should be shared in your speech. If time is limited, focus only on the key points and even consider skipping secondary ones.

5. **Engage the Audience:**

- **Q&A Sessions:** If you have some extra time during the presentation, reserve a bit of that to answer your audience's questions. This allows attendees to discuss specific matters, ask for clarification, and provide their views, stimulating meaningful discussion.

- **Interactive features:** Add depth and participation by including opportunities for feedback in the form of quick polls, short group discussions, or audience interaction. The latter presents attendees with chances to really participate in the discussion and keep them interested. The use of interactive elements can increase the audience's comprehension of your message and reinforce key information.

Chapter Summary

- Public speakers employ different methods to deliver their messages to their diverse audiences. These could be in the form of manuscript speech, memorized speech, impromptu speech, or extemporaneous speech.

- Speakers should discover their styles and stick with them in order to perpetuate their brands. To find one's delivery style, it is important to undertake self-assessment, audience analysis, and to embrace criticism for ongoing professional development.

- Public speakers should cultivate the habit of periodically practicing or rehearsing their speeches to achieve a certain level of perfection.

- One issue every speaker struggles with, irrespective of their level of experience in the industry, is time. It is imperative that they should devise a way to properly manage their time. For every event they participate in, speakers need to know their time limits and consequently plan their speech delivery to fit into their scheduled duration.

Quiz

1. How many types of speeches do we have based on the different delivery styles?

    a. 3
    b. 7
    c. 4

2. The type of speech delivery that involves reading the content of the script in verbatim is referred to as the _____

    a. Manuscript speech
    b. Impromptu speech
    c. Extemporaneous speech

3. Speech contents that are mostly recited from memory and not from written notes are a typical example of _____ .

    a. Memorized speech
    b. Manuscript speech
    c. Impromptu speech

4. When a public speaker delivers a speech off-the-cuff or without reading directly from the script, the speech delivery style is called _____ .

    a. Manuscript speech
    b. Impromptu speech
    c. Memorized speech

5. To discover their most convenient speech delivery style, speakers need to assess their strengths and weaknesses as far as presenting a speech is concerned.

   a. False
   b. True

6. Speakers must undertake audience analysis for these purposes except _____ .

   a. To fully understand the audience's preferences.
   b. To know how to best engage with them.
   c. To know if they like funny jokes.

7. The easiest way for a speaker to identify which speech delivery styles work best for them is to review the specific delivery style used in his/her past speeches.

   a. True
   b. False

8. The main problem associated with memorized speeches is that the _____ .

   a. The speaker may be stuck in the middle of his/her delivery
   b. The speaker doesn't need to prepare for the speech presentation
   c. The audience doesn't usually like a memorized speaker.

9. To master their art of speech delivery, it is important that speakers practice regularly and form the habit of paying serious attention to the important details in their speeches.

   a. False
   b. True

10. The speeches given verbatim at the political or election rallies are examples of a _____ .

    a. Memorized speech
    b. Manuscript speech
    c. Impromptu speech

Answer Key

1 – c	2 – a	3 – a	4 – b	5 – b
6 – c	7 – a	8 – a	9 – b	10 – b

CHAPTER 8

Effective Use of Voice

Key Learning Objectives

- Understand the role of tone, pitch, and volume.
- Explore the techniques for improving vocal delivery
- Learn how to manage nervousness and speak with clarity

What Makes Your Voice Powerful?

Let me ask you something: **Do you love your voice?** Or are you among the 70% of people who say, *"I don't like how I sound"*?

If you're in that majority, here's something to reflect on: Your voice is not just sound. It's your identity.

Your voice is like a musical instrument—just like a pianist knows which key to press to create harmony, you must learn which tone, pace, and pause to use to create an impact.

And guess what?

Every time you speak—whether it's one-on-one, on a Zoom call, or on the stage in a boardroom—you are practicing public speaking. Every conversation is a performance, and all speaking is public speaking.

In my case, it all started at a call center. I didn't have a fancy degree or a big network—all I had was my voice. Every sale I made, every connection I built, every door I opened—it was because I learned how to use my voice with power.

"Thank you for calling RCI. How may I help you today?"

This one statement was just not a question, but the verbal attributes, which included my clear pronunciation, right tone, steady rate of speech, and meaningful pitch in my voice, that made the entire call into a win-win stance.

So here's my message to you:

Love your voice. Own it. Train it. Respect it. Because when you do, your voice won't just be heard, it will be remembered.

If I could build my life around my voice, so can you!

In this chapter, we will talk about the effective uses of voice in public speaking.

8.1 The Role of Tone, Pitch, and Volume

In public speaking, your voice isn't just a tool; it's the melody that transforms words into emotions and ideas into impact.

So, how resonant is your voice?

Are you a passionate speaker?

How powerful is your voice compared to other speakers?

What is it about your voice that makes you stand out from other speakers?

As a public speaker, the best way to distinguish yourself from the rest in the business is the effective use of your voice, specifically your tone, rate, pitch, and articulation.[32] How you combine these voice attributes can have a resounding influence on your ability to communicate well and get your audience fully engaged, which might earn you a place among the highly rated public speakers.

Figure 8.1 Use of voice

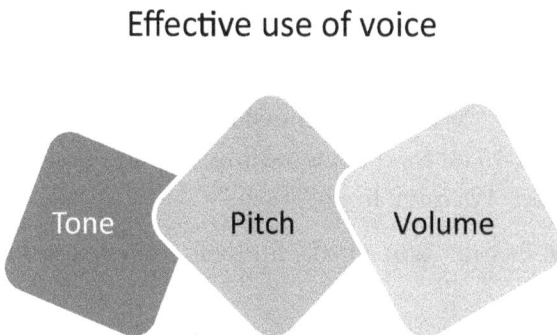

Effective use of voice

Tone · Pitch · Volume

---

32. Renee Grant-Williams, Voice Power: Using Your Voice to Captivate, Persuade, and Command Attention (New York, Amacom, 2022) 75-80.

Let us consider these three important attributes, one after the other, with a few examples:

8.1.1 Tone

Every person has their own natural and unique tone with which they deliver content to their listeners. This tone is very crucial to their audience because of its uniqueness and identity. As a speaker, your tone is the mood or emotion behind how your voice sounds in the ear of your listeners. The mood behind your tone will help you establish credibility, trust, and engagement with the audience. Your tone could range from someone who is not so sure about something to a person who is enthusiastic, serious, warm, or an authority on the topic under discussion.

Examples: The following examples demonstrate how a speaker's tone can reveal different levels of emotion and commitment when talking to others:

1. **Enthusiasm:** If you are a marketer presenting a new product on behalf of your company, an enthusiastic tone can generate excitement and interest in a potential buyer.

    Scenario: You're telling a friend about a new restaurant.

    Example: "You won't believe how amazing this new place is! The food is incredible, and the vibe is just perfect. We have to go!"

    Why: Enthusiasm sparks interest and excitement in others.

2. **Empathy:** If you get an opportunity to resolve conflicts and your voice can demonstrate empathy for others'

feelings, consider this statement: "I understand this resolution might be challenging for both parties, but this is the only route we must all tread towards a lasting peace between our communities." This shows empathy and builds trust on both sides.

Scenario: A friend is upset about a tough day at work.

Example: "I can imagine how frustrating that must have been for you. I'm here if you want to talk about it."

Why: Empathy shows understanding and builds trust.

3. **Authority:** Imagine yourself as a team leader who is to present your findings about an issue in a business meeting; using a confident and authoritative tone when presenting your results can earn you some respect. For example, *"Based on our analysis and our past experiences on similar issues, this company should proceed with our strategy because of ABCD…."* This statement displays confidence in your proposal and, at the same time, makes you sound like an authority.

Scenario: You're explaining a group project's plan to classmates.

Example: "We've reviewed all the options, and the best approach is to divide the tasks this way to meet the deadline."

Why: A confident tone establishes credibility and leadership.

Exercise: Practice Your Tone for Effective Communication

This exercise helps you master tone modulation for different situations.

Step 1: Read this Sentence Aloud

"What time will you be coming back?"

Step 2: Imagine Saying This to Different People

- **Best Friend:**
  - Casual, relaxed tone, possibly playful.
  - Example: *"Hey, what time are you coming back? Got plans for later!"*

- **Spouse/Partner:**
  - Warm, caring tone with a touch of curiosity.
  - Example: *"What time will you be back, love? Should I keep dinner ready?"*

- **Boss:**
  - Polite, formal tone, showing respect.
  - Example: *"Excuse me, sir/ma'am, what time should I expect you back?"*

- **Stranger:**
  - Neutral tone, maintaining professionalism or politeness.
  - Example: *"Could you please let me know what time you'll be back?"*

Step 3: Record Yourself

Use your phone to record each version. This will help you identify areas to improve.

Step 4: Rate Yourself (Scale: 1 to 6)

After listening to your recordings, rate yourself on the following:

1. **Voice Relevance:**
   - Did your tone vary appropriately based on who you were addressing?

2. **Confidence:**
   - Did you sound sure of yourself?
   - Was there hesitation or loss of volume at the end of sentences?

3. **Stuttering:**
   - Did you repeat or trip over any syllables?

4. **Clarity:**
   - Was your speech clear?
   - Could every word be easily understood?

5. **Speed:**
   - Did your pace suit each situation? Were you too fast or too slow?

6. **Resonance:**
   - Did your voice sound full and expressive, or was it flat and monotone?

Step 5: Repeat for 30 Days

Practice daily and score yourself consistently. This works even better if you do it with a partner or coach for feedback.

Another important exercise would be to say the same sentences with different emotions, like being happy, sad, angry, excited, and jealous.

This is a very good practice to understand your emotions with your voice and evaluate yourself on vocal variety.

Use this exercise for different sentences to expand your versatility! For example:

- *"How was your day?"*
- *"Can you explain this to me?"*

This will make you more adaptable and impactful in real-life conversations.

8.1.2 Pitch

Which singer in the world has a high pitch?

Example: Mariah Carey, Christina Aguilera, Prince, Whitney Houston

Which Singer has a very low pitch?

Example: Michael Jackson, Aretha Franklin, Sam Cooke, Otis Redding, Ray Charles, Stevie Wonder

This refers to how high or low your voice sounds, and it is very important that you are self-aware of this as a public speaker. You can vary your pitch to emphasize key points, create interest, and evoke emotions to make your speech more engaging. However, the pitch variation and the important points to be emphasized depend on your audience, the context, and the environment. This is because you may not necessarily use the same pitch to deliver your message if you were to speak to a different audience residing in different locations.

The most important thing is to know your audience, their requirements, and the best method (pitch variation) you can use to carry them along, from the start of your talk to the end. Most great public speakers use a rising pitch at the end of a sentence to ask a question or use a lower pitch to convey authority or seriousness. Doing this helps them prevent monotony and maintain audience engagement.

Let us consider other ways you can use your pitch to communicate with your audience:

1. **Emphasis:** Raising your pitch slightly when highlighting a key point can make it stand out. For example, if you want to draw your audience's attention to the word "quality" in the following sentence, you can say, "*The most important aspect is quality.*" It is usually advisable to have a short break before you pronounce the word "*quality*" with a bit higher or lower pitch.

2. **Excitement:** Imagine if, in the middle of your speech, you decided to give a tip and you came up with this statement: "*I'm so excited to share this news with you!*" This makes your excitement contagious, and your audience will be willing to know what is next.

3. **Seriousness:** You can communicate the seriousness or significance of a situation by lowering your pitch and using a solemn expression. A good example is the pitch of how one would say, "*We need to address this issue immediately.*"

4. **Storytelling:** Varying your pitch when telling a story can make it more compelling. For example, "*And then, out of nowhere, the solution appeared!*" Speakers can use pitch variation to build suspense and interest.

8.1.3 Volume

This is how loud or soft your voice is. Your volume helps to control the intensity and clarity of your message and also helps to emphasize points and create a dramatic effect. Effective use of your voice's volume can help you command attention, emphasize points, and ensure your message is heard clearly. Most public speakers use either a loud or soft voice to emphasize key points or create excitement, intimacy, or suspense. In short, effective use of your voice's volume can also prevent monotony and keep the audience engaged.

Let's see a few instances where a speaker's voice volume can make it possible for them to build trust and increase engagement with their audience.

1. **Commanding Attention:** As a public speaker, it is always good to start your speech with a strong and confident volume to capture your audience's attention immediately within the first few minutes of your introduction. For example: *"Welcome everyone, thank you for being here today!"* This sets the tone for an engaging presentation and for the audience to come along interestingly.

2. **Building Anticipation:** One of the ways to attract your audience's attention and create a sense of anticipation is to lower your voice's volume. Doing this will make them lean in to hear the full details. For example, *"Are you aware that the secret to our success is..."*

3. **Clarity:** Maintaining a clear and consistent voice volume ensures your message is understood. In a large room, speaking loudly enough for everyone to hear prevents misunderstandings and keeps your audience engaged.

8.1.4 Integrating Tone, Pitch, and Volume for Mastery:

1. **Practice and Feedback:** Professional public speakers grow through consistent practice, putting deliberate efforts into sharpening their speaking skills and acting on constructive feedback they receive from their audiences, mentors, and peers. These are typically lifelong activities every successful speaker today has been undertaking. Your mentors and contemporaries can significantly help you refine your pitch, tone, and volume. Another practical way to handle this is to constantly record your speeches, analyze your methods of speech delivery, and work on improving any areas that show certain weaknesses in your tone, volume, and pitch.

2. **Awareness and Adaptation:** Great speakers always pay close attention to the nature of their audiences, knowing who they are, what they want, and how best to serve them. It is a fact that, based on the composition and requirements of an audience, a professional speaker should adapt their tone, pitch, and volume to carry their audience along. It is unhelpful, even arrogant, to use a high pitch and too vibrant tone when speaking to a small group of professionals who already have deep knowledge about your topic but just require a little motivation. A soft, appealing tone with low volume will be enough to boost their morale as far as refocusing their minds on the topic.

3. **Breathing and Relaxation:** Nervousness is one of the main issues public speakers need to deal with. The good news is that many have overcome it, and you, too, can. One of the simple ways to do so is to practice

proper breathing techniques that will help you maintain a steady and calm voice. You need to practice deep breathing exercises once in a while, even if you do not have any speaking engagements, to reduce nervousness.

4. **Engagement and Interaction:** Asking questions or telling relevant stories at the beginning, middle, or end of your speech using the right tone, pitch, and volume will usually attract the attention of your audience. Asking questions, especially, will give you the chance to incorporate pauses and make your speech more dynamic and interactive.

5. **Authenticity:** Authenticity resonates with audiences because no one enjoys people faking things. So be genuine in your delivery. If you are African, Asian, or British, speak English like one. This is because many in the audience may know you more than you thought. It is always good to use your natural pitch, tone, and volume to connect with people on a personal level.

8.2 Techniques for Improving Vocal Delivery

Since man has learned to gather as a community, society, or an association, there have been famous men and women who are orators, addressing community issues with their authoritative vocal delivery.

Modern-day public speakers are not in any way different than the orators in several communities, utilizing their voice as a powerful tool to help their audience solve many problems. Therefore, it is important, as a public speaker, to use or manage your voice effectively to convey your message understandably and convincingly.

I have highlighted a few techniques below to improve your vocal delivery as a professional public speaker.

Figure 8.2 Improving vocal delivery

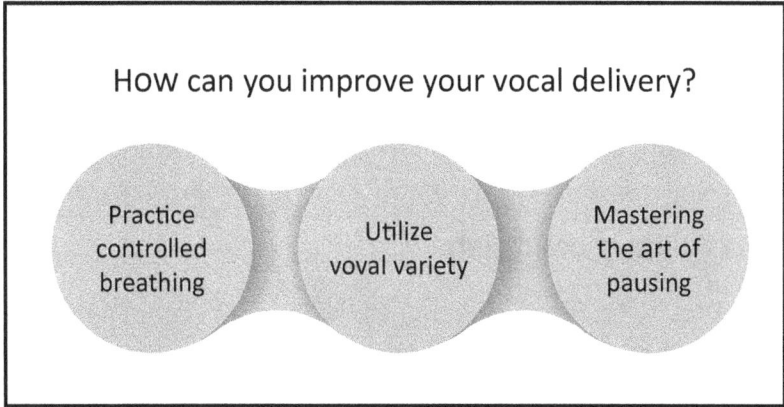

How can you improve your vocal delivery?

Practice controlled breathing

Utilize voval variety

Mastering the art of pausing

8.2.1 Practice Controlled Breathing

Your ability to control how you breathe is the foundation of strong vocal delivery. It has a way of helping you maintain clarity, a steady voice, and reduced anxiety, and it allows you to better project what to say next.

Take the following two strategic steps to control your breathing and boost your vocal delivery.

- **Diaphragmatic Breathing:** You can do this by breathing deeply from your diaphragm rather than shallowly from your chest. When you breathe in, your abdomen should expand while your chest remains almost still. You can assist yourself by placing one hand on your abdomen and the other on your chest as a guide. As a good practice, even if you are not the type who gets easily nervous to speak, always take deep breaths before starting your speech and between sentences. This method will not only calm your nerves but also give you the power to project your voice effectively in a way that your audience will understand your points. Remember that the reason you are given the opportunity to speak is to be understood clearly.

- **Pace Your Speech:** Try your best to pace your speech so that it doesn't appear rushed. In other words, delivering your speech between breaths can give you the opportunity to speak coherently and confidently.

8.2.2 Utilize Vocal Variety

As the saying goes, "variety is the spice of life". Therefore, practice how to meaningfully vary your voice to keep your audience engaged. By doing so, you will be able to emphasize each key point in your speech to encourage better comprehension on the part of your audience. Without variation, your voice can become monotonous, causing listeners to lose interest.

Pitch Variation: Vary the pitch of your voice to reflect the emotional content of your speech. Use a higher pitch for excitement or questioning, and a lower pitch for authority or seriousness. Another good example is when telling a story, use a lower pitch to describe the storyline and a higher pitch to reveal the lessons learnt. This contrast will make your story more engaging and memorable.

8.2.3 Master the Art of Pausing

Pausing is a powerful technique that can add emphasis, give your audience time to absorb information, and help you maintain control of your speech. Remember, pausing is what we naturally do when we drink water during a meal. We pause and drink to allow the food to settle down, and then another serving follows. In practice, a pause intermittently allows your audience to digest the key points in your speech for a few seconds before you serve them the next point. Though pausing should not be done for too long, otherwise your audience may become weary. You can learn to do this in 5 to 10 seconds.

TIP

Two pause techniques you should definitely give a try!

1. **Emphasis Pauses:** This is when you pause briefly after making an important statement to let it sink in. This gives your words greater impact on the listeners' ears.

2. **Transition Pauses:** You use this technique when you want to transition between points to give your audience a moment to process earlier points and prepare them for what is coming next. It also helps them reflect or write down a few things.

8.3 Managing Nervousness and Speaking Clearly

Nervousness is a common psychological "malaise" that every human being has been battling with since time immemorial, from the strongest to the feeblest man. Everyone experiences nervousness at one time or another.

Every human body, in response to perceived or imagined threat, prepares itself to either fight or flee, which most times leads to a faster heartbeat, increased blood pressure, and profuse sweating, among others.

> **FUN FACT**
>
> ### Basic Truth about Nervousness
>
> It is both a natural and personal way of responding to a new experience or a situation outside your comfort zone. Nervousness is like a bully; it hates being confronted. Once you make up your mind to face it headlong, you will discover that it is just a temporary, uncomfortable feeling.

The fear of public speaking is the single most common phobia experienced by approximately 75% of people globally. That means you are not alone.

The only proven way to overcome your fear of public speaking is to shift the attention from yourself. Even the most confident speakers find ways to distance themselves from their audience. The reality is that the nightmarish scenarios you envision may not eventually come true.

The truth is that you cannot eliminate your nervousness, but you can manage or reduce it to the barest level with some simple relaxation exercises or other tips we shall consider below.

1. **Prepare:** Even if you are not invited to speak, always be prepared. And the more material you gather, the more you will be able to master and handle all aspects of your presentation.

2. **Practice:** Once you have prepared enough materials for your talk, it is time to practice. You *must* practice early and regularly. This will empower you to confidently do whatever it takes to motivate, educate, and encourage your audience.

3. **Familiarity:** Try as much as possible to get familiar with the environment or venue of the presentation by arriving earlier. It may earn you some confidence. Also, free your mind by engaging in conversation with one or two people hanging around the venue. You will be surprised by how this little tip can cause your nervousness to gradually fade away.

4. **Accompany Yourself:** Ask a friend, colleague, mentee, or your spouse to accompany you to the event. Let them sit at a strategic location so that you can easily gaze at them once in a while and draw some encouragement from that. This is the secret of many university professors who attend speaking events with their master's and doctoral students.

5. **The Audience Are Your Friends:** Assure yourself that you are neither in the camp of your enemies nor held hostage by the audience. They see you as superior or as a colleague whom they want to learn from. Hence, they are your friends.

6. **Listen to Music:** Get yourself your favorite music and fill your mind with positive thoughts or energy. Also, look for good motivational talks that can help boost your morale. Do this regularly, within days and a few hours of your presentation.

7. **Put the Pressure Elsewhere:** The first two to five minutes are a very crucial moment for you to handle your nervousness while you are on the stage. When the pressure of nervousness sets in, do not absorb it; rather, shift the pressure elsewhere, possibly to your audience. Ask one or two relevant questions from the audience and get random answers from different people, even if the first person has answered them

correctly. In this way, you are creating a friendly atmosphere between you and your audience while stabilizing yourself mentally.

8. **Carefully Choose What You Consume:** It is good to avoid caffeine because of its epinephrine effect, which can cause your heart to race quickly or restrict blood circulation in some parts of your body. Avoid salty foods, too, so that your mouth will not easily become dry on your presentation day. Do not fast or eat heavy food on the presentation day to keep yourselves light and vivacious.

9. **Water:** Water, they say, is life. You need a bottle or a cup of water readily beside you. Drinking some water while delivering a speech can help calm down your nerves.

10. **Breathing Exercise:** Practice alternate nostril breathing technique: You will need your thumb, your pinkie finger, and your nose for this exercise. You can start simply by covering your left nostril with your left thumb and slowly and deeply inhaling for about 10 seconds. Then, almost immediately, cover your right nostril with your left pinkie finger, while keeping your left nostril pressed closed. Your mouth must remain closed at all times during the exercise. Again, hold for 5–10 seconds. Then remove your left thumb from your left nostril and slowly exhale for a count of 10. Wait for a few seconds and repeat the same technique.

Chapter Summary

- The way public speakers use their voices by effectively controlling their voices' pitch, tone, and volume can greatly influence their speech delivery. In the age of personal branding, every public speaker should focus on controlling their voice's tone, pitch, and volume to become quite recognizable by the audience.

- It takes regular practice, self-awareness, and incorporating feedback for speakers to be able to control their voices' pitch, volume, and tone.

- Some of the well-known techniques for improving vocal delivery include, but are not limited to, practicing controlled breathing, employing pitch variations, and mastering the art of pausing.

- Some steps public speakers can take to actively manage their nervousness and speak clearly to their audience include allocating more time to preparation, constantly practicing, taking good care of their health, engaging in breathing exercises, and learning how to make their profession appear less stressful. They can do this by liking their audience more and focusing on the benefits (both social and financial) of being a public speaker.

Quiz

1. The three attributes of a speaker's voice are _____ .
    a. Tone, pitch, and volume
    b. Volume, speed, and tone
    c. Pitch, speed, and tempo

2. Depending on a speaker's objectives, whether to emphasize key points, create interest, or evoke the audience's emotions, the speaker can decide to increase or lower his/her pitch.
    a. True
    b. False

3. There are different types of tones. What is the most appropriate tone a speaker can use to make people act quickly?
    a. An urgent tone
    b. An empathetic tone
    c. A sincere tone

4. How high or low a speaker's voice sounds is referred to as his/her _____
    a. Tone
    b. Pitch
    c. Volume

5. What is the best advice for a new speaker trying to master the impact of his voice's pitch, tone, and volume?

   a. The speaker should record, analyze his voice, and improve his voice attributes.

   b. The speaker should use a fake voice when delivering a speech.

   c. The speaker shouldn't bother about receiving feedback on his voice's quality.

6. As discussed in this chapter, the two common pause techniques are _____

   a. Emphatic and transition pauses

   b. Pitch and tone pauses

   c. Speaker and audience pauses

7. The kind of pause technique often utilized by speakers when they want to move from one key point to another is _____

   a. Emphatic pause

   b. Transition pause

   c. Loud pause

8. The process of changing one's voice pitch based on the emotions to be expressed in a speech content is referred to as _____

   a. High pitch

   b. Low pitch

   c. Pitch variation

9. _____ is the practice of breathing deeply from one's diaphragm rather than shallowly from one's chest.

   a. Powerful breathing
   b. Diaphragm breathing
   c. Short breathing

10. Nervousness is both a natural and personal way of responding to a new experience or a situation outside one's comfort zone.

   a. True
   b. False

Answer Key

1 – a	2 – a	3 – a	4 – b	5 – a
6 – a	7 – b	8 – c	9 – b	10 – a

CHAPTER 9

Body Language and Gestures

Key Learning Objectives

- Learn the importance of nonverbal communication
- Understand the effective use of gestures
- Master how to maintain eye contact
- Exploring confidence poses

Body language and gestures in public speaking are like seasoning in a dish—without them, even the best content can feel bland. The right gestures add flavor, enhance impact, and make your message memorable, just like spices bring a dish to life!

According to Albert Mehrabian's famous study, only 7% of communication is verbal (words), while **38% is vocal tone** and **55% is body language.** So, how you say something matters more than what you say![33]

---

33. "Your Words Only Tell a Fraction of the Story — Here's Why Tone and Body Language Actually Matter More", *Entrepreneur*, February 27, 2025, https://www.entrepreneur.com/leadership/your-words-only-tell-a-fraction-of-the-story-heres-why/485004,

In this chapter, we shall be exploring the importance of nonverbal communication, effective use of gestures, maintaining eye contact, and confidence poses as veritable tools of communication in public speaking.

9.1 Importance of Nonverbal Communication

An excellent way of communicating effectively while addressing a public gathering is through the use of body language and gestures. This is also referred to as nonverbal communication. It is, however, very pertinent to highlight some of the benefits of nonverbal communication.

9.1.1 Advantages of non-verbal communication:

1. **Garnering attention:** Body language and gestures encourage the audience to pay rapt attention to the speaker and enhance their understanding of the subject matter. Facial expressions, body movements, hand dexterity, gesticulation, and postures combined with a small smile will naturally evoke smiles from listeners, while your speech will simultaneously provide deeper meaning and understanding to the audience.

2. **Building confidence and trust:** The use of body language and gestures that appropriately suit the purpose of the discussion can help the audience build trust and confidence in the speaker. The level of movement and charisma put in place while elaborating on some important points on a topic, with an effective use of facial expressions and gestures, can cause the audience to have confidence and trust in the speaker.

3. **Expression of emotions and feelings:** It is imperative to let people know that some events and situations are very difficult to put in plain words without

proper description. Therefore, the only way to show the emotional gravity of the message that is being passed across to the audience is by using nonverbal communication in conjunction with the speech. Body language and gestures provide more information that expresses the emotion of the speaker, which may be difficult to put into words.

4. **Showcasing the intelligence level and understanding of the speaker:** An intelligent speaker would always utilize appropriate body language with essential gesticulation to show the magnitude of their knowledge and understanding of the subject matter. This, invariably, will propel the audience into a complete understanding of the topic under discussion.

5. **Promoting verbal communication:** Most often, body language and gestures also promote verbal communication, as they help the speaker to creatively describe some important points in his/her speech. For example, maintaining good eye contact with the audience helps the speaker to assess the level of understanding of the listeners and gives him the opportunity to buttress his points.

6. **Gives room for quick communication:** As a matter of fact, all orators demonstrate or display certain observable body language or gestures that are highly responsive and faster than verbal communication. For instance, winking of eyes with a snap of fingers connotes urgency in action.

7. **Helps to promote interpersonal relationships:** Nonverbal communication can engender better interpersonal relationships and foster understanding between the audience and the speaker. When the crowd or spectator responds to nonverbal cues, it indicates

that the audience is listening and understanding the speaker very well. An occasional interlude of silence with eye contact and appropriate hand gestures can give the audience the opportunity to reason together among themselves and also foster relationships among the listeners.

8. **Helpful in communicating crafty and subtle messages:** Some events are better expressed with nonverbal communication without creating a threat to anyone. For instance, holding one's lips could mean keeping quiet or silent without actually shouting at anybody to do so.

9. **Nonverbal communication creates synergy and an engaging atmosphere:** The synergy involved in nonverbal communication is overwhelmingly great, as it allows groups of people to share opinions and ideas and thereby create an engaging atmosphere for the audience. The people will really want to imitate the speaker's eye contact, gestures, and postures, therefore giving room for the exchange of ideas and beliefs and resulting in bridging cultural differences.

10. **Nonverbal communication is also advantageous in a noisy environment:** In a large crowd where a public address system is not available, the most effective way to communicate is by using body language or hand gestures such as waving hands, eye contact, straight posture, holding of lips, etc., to maintain decorum. Therefore, it is easier to use nonverbal communication for a better understanding of the message in a noisy environment.

9.2. Effective Use of Gestures

Gesture is one of the types of nonverbal communication. Others include facial expression, paralinguistics, body language, eye gaze or eye contact, haptics (touch), proxemics or personal space, appearance, and artifacts (objects and images).

Before gestures can be effectively used, it is essential to understand their meanings, types, and interpretations of such gestures.

9.2.1 Meanings of Gestures

A gesture can be described as any form of movement displayed during speaking that may provide an avenue to support the information or idea that is not readily expressed in speech. It may involve hand movement simultaneously used with verbal communication and facial expression to emphasize crucial words.

In ancient times, early human beings depended largely on nonverbal communication as their primary communication tool before the development of language.

Large amounts of information are exchanged through gestures and body language, which are the two primary modes of nonverbal communication.

Gestures provide additional information to help the audience understand the speaker's intentions and prevent a language barrier. It is another useful way to express oneself without telling people what one wants to say. However, gesture plays a supportive role when speech adequately portrays or describes the speaker's goals.[34]

---

34. Derek Borthwick, *Body Language How To Read Any Body: The Secret To Nonverbal Communication To Understand & Influence In, Business, Sales, Online, Presenting & Public Speaking, Healthcare, Attraction & Seduction* (Amazon, 2021) 102-133.

9.2.2 Types of Gestures

There are seven main types of gestures.

1. **Adaptors**

    Adaptors involve touching behaviors and movement to show how you feel internally, which may involve arousal or anxiety. It is a resultant effect of subconsciousness, uneasiness, anxiety, and strange feelings in one's subconscious. Or being unable to control one's environment. Adaptors could be self-focused or object-focused, that is, touching oneself subconsciously or fiddling with objects. Common self-adaptors include scratching the body, twirling hair, fidgeting with fingers, or rubbing hands against each other.

    However, examples of object-focused adaptors include fiddling with phones or pens to ease anxiety, playing with a straw in a drink, or peeling the label off a bottle of drink.

2. **Emblems**

    These are gestures that have a specific, planned meaning. These are kinds of body movements that express a specific meaning without the need for words to describe them. Emblems are unique and specific depending on the environment's cultural and linguistic influence or contexts, which makes them clear and deliberate, like any spoken word. Common examples of emblematic gestures include waving of hands to signify "hello" or "goodbye." A head nod to indicate "yes," whereas shaking of head side-to-side means "no." You may raise your finger to your lips or use your finger to hold your lips to indicate "be quiet or silent."

3. Illustrators or Iconic Gestures

These are very commonly used when verbally describing events or situations accompanied by gestures or hand movements to add appropriate meaning to your speech. Oftentimes, verbal messages are explained with hand gestures to convey the information explicitly. For example, hand gestures can be used to describe the size and shape of an object. You might pinch your fingers close together to symbolize that it is "small" or flatten your hand to show that its surface is "smooth." Iconic gestures or illustrators are largely involuntary and seemingly natural gestures that help in thinking and brainstorming an idea.

4. Metaphoric Gestures

These are used to represent abstract concepts. Although they are closely related to illustrators, they are less literal and often susceptible to interpretation. For instance, stacking hands on top of one another to explain overlapping ideas is a metaphoric gesture. Balancing of hands like a scale to indicate weighing two options or opinions is another example.

5. Deictic Gestures

These kinds of gestures are very vital to communication and also the easiest to understand. They are often used to point out a person, an object, or a direction of reference. For example, pointing a finger at an object to indicate emphasis or direction.

6. Manipulator Gestures

These involve the unconscious use of hands to manipulate other parts of the body or an object without any direct correlation with the speech. It is always very difficult to assign a specific meaning to a manipulator gesture without proper context because the action or movement may not correlate with the meaning of the speech. For example, covering your mouth when you are amazed or shocked, resting your chin while meditating, or tapping your foot when you are in a hurry or feeling impatient.

7. **Beat Gestures**

These gestures follow the rhythm, pacing, and cadence of a speaker's speech but do not necessarily describe the speech content. Examples of beat gestures are up-and-down movements of hands to emphasize some of the speaker's words. However, unlike iconic gestures, it does not refer to a specific word or object but practically emphasizes the whole statement made by the speaker.

9.2.3 Classifications of Gestures

Although there are seven main types of gestures, all the types mentioned earlier can be categorized under one of these four classes of gesture:

1. **Emphatic Gestures:** These involve communicating the emotions and feelings of the speaker.

Figure 9.1 Example of Emphatic Gesture

Source: (Stablediffusionweb.com, 2025)[35]

2. **Descriptive Gestures:** These describe the events or
   situations as they apply to the subject matter.

---

35. "Emphatic gestures", Stablediffusionweb.com, accessed 5 July, 2025,
https://stablediffusionweb.com/ja/prompts/emphatic-gestures

| Figure 9.2 | **Example of descriptive gesture** |

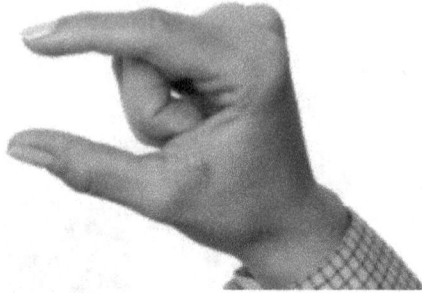

(Source: Makesafetyfun.com, 2025)[36]

3. **Suggestive Gestures:** These merely indicate the mood, impression, or opinion formed about the topic.

| Figure 9.3 | **Example of suggestive gestures** |

(Source: Scienceofpeople, 2025)[37]

---

36. "Add Life To Your Safety Talks With Descriptive Gestures," accessed 17 June, 2025, https://www.makesafetyfun.com/add-life-to-your-safety-talks-with-descriptive-gestures/

37. "60 Hand Gestures You Should Be Using and Their Meaning", accessed May 10 May, 2025, Scienceofpeoplehttps://www.scienceofpeople.com/hand-gestures/

4. **Prompting Gestures:** These involve acting as quick directives or instructions.

Figure 9.4 **Example of a prompt gesture**

(Source: Playstreet, 2025)[38]

9.2.4 Interpretations of Gestures

Interpreting gestures depends on general acceptability or public approval. Although this is somehow difficult owing to cultural differences, some of these gestures, as agreed upon by the American Sign Language (ASL), are generally interpreted as follows:

---

38. "Prompts in Special Education", Playstreet, accessed 15 June, 2025, https://images.app.goo.gl/PsgJ62qHiEWH37X76

| Table 9.1 | **Types and interpretations of gestures** |

Gesture	Interpretation
Thumb-up[39]	Interpreted as approved or acceptance
Thumb-down[40]	Means disapproval or rejection
Pointing of the finger[41]	Indicates direction or emphasis

39. "Why Does a Thumbs-Up Gesture Mean "okay"?".Guernseydonkey.com, accessed 1 June, 2025, https://extra.guernseydonkey.com/why-does-a-thumbs-up-gesture-mean-okay/

40. "Thumb down", emojiterra.com, accessed 5 July, 2025, https://emojiterra.com/thumbs-down/

41. "Download Finger Pointing Left transparent PNG", Stick PNG, accessed 1 July, 2025, https://www.stickpng.com/img/people/fingers/finger-pointing-left#google_vignette

Gesture	Interpretation
Waving[42]	Signals greeting or farewell
Nodding of the head[43] Nod your head (yes) Shake your head (no)	Interpreted as acceptance or approval
Shaking head side-to-side (shown above)	Means disapproval
Hugging or petting[44]	Means appreciation/affection

42. "Waving Hand", Adobe Stock, accessed 1 July, 2025, https://stock.adobe.com/jp/search?k=%2Fwaving+hand

43. "Do you nod your head?" Peoples Daily, accessed 2 July, 2025, https://www.peoplesdailyng.com/do-you-nod-your-head/

44. "People hugghing Images," Freepik, accessed 3 July, 2025, https://www.freepik.com/free-photos-vectors/people-hugging

Gesture	Interpretation
Resting of head on the palm of your hand[45]	It can be interpreted as being in distress about something.
Folding of arms at chest level[46]	Means fear
Eye contact[47]	Means confidence, attentiveness, and engagement.

---

45. "Palm Forehead Images, Pictures And Stock Photos", Greamstime, accessed 3 July, 2025, https://www.dreamstime.com/photos-images/palm-forehead.html

46. "What Arm Gestures Convey", http://Westsidetoastmasters.com, accessed 4 July, 2025, https://westsidetoastmasters.com/resources/book_of_body_language/chap4.html

47. "Eye contact icon Generic Thin Outline Color", Freepik, accessed 3 July, 2025, https://www.freepik.com/icon/eye-contact_5687610

9.2.5 How to Use Gestures Effectively

For the effective use of gestures, the following approaches must be considered:

1. **Uphold good eye contact:** Eye contact plays an important role in communication, and it is very impactful. A steady eye contact generally indicates attentiveness, focus, sincerity, and confidence. Although it must not be excessively prolonged, it can take turns from one person to another among the audience. However, avoiding eye contact could indicate discomfort, shyness, or dishonesty.

2. **Head nodding or tilting the head to the side:** This shows that you are focused and listening respectfully; it also indicates that you agree with what the speaker is saying. It can be used to acknowledge valid opinions and thoughts. It is an impressive gesture to determine the level of assimilation, acceptance, and approval of the topic. A head nod with a little smile shows that you are engaged with enthusiasm.

3. **Open palms:** Speakers should effectively engage their audience with this positive gesture. Open palms symbolize acceptance, effectiveness, trustworthiness, and honesty.

4. **Open arms:** Gesturing with open arms makes the speaker appear more welcoming or accepting. The speaker's hands must be free and not folded at the chest as if they are feeling cold, unsafe, or panicked. This could indicate a defensive approach and fear.

5. **Smiling:** Occasional smiles during communication make the speech fascinating, attractive, and emphatic about the speaker's confidence and intelligence level. However, this must be appropriately balanced depending on the speech content. You can't be smiling while speaking about a bad situation or story.

6. **Upright and open posture:** A speaker must stand straight with the trunk of their body open, which indicates openness, trustworthiness, transparency, and confidence.

7. **Firm handshake:** A firm handshake and warm greeting motivate the audience and build their confidence and interpersonal relationship with respect.

8. **Avoid folding of hands:** Folding of hands together symbolizes nervousness and defense as well as a lack of confidence. If a speaker lacks confidence and authority, who will believe his/her words?

9. **Leaning in while speaking:** It's a very good approach to indicate that the speaker is comfortable and is interested in having a conversation with the listeners. However, other people's personal space should not be improperly invaded.

10. **Hand gestures should be used to add emphasis to the speech:** The importance of gesticulation is to lay emphasis on very vital points in a speech.

11. **Persuasive hand gesture is very essential:** Another gesture that is highly essential in public speaking, if used effectively, is a persuasive hand gesture. This involves positioning your hands in a praying position with the tips of your fingers touching each other.

12. **Memorization by hand gestures:** Doing hand gestures while trying to memorize some important information or recall certain points can be very effective. However, for effective use of hand gestures, the following negative gestures should be avoided:

- Rapid blinking of the eye
- Lip biting
- Face touching

- Hands on chest
- Head in hands
- Cross arms
- Cross legs
- Hands in pocket
- Speaking rapidly
- Frowning face

TIP

Generally, people usually associate cross or negative signs with negative gestures, and public speakers should be fully aware of these and the negative implications of such on their audience.

Table 9.2 **Positive body language Vs. Negative body language**

Positive Body Language	Negative Body Language
How to say "I like you"	Are you guilty of these sins? Avoid them, and people will respond more positively to you.
• Direct eye contact (no staring) • Warm, open smile (teeth revealed) • Nodding • Head tilted • Open, inclusive gestures (palms showing • Fully facing others • Leaning forward	• Not making eye contact • Tight or no smile • Down and away glances • Not fully facing, at an angle • Leaning away • Hunched shoulders • Too-stiff posture • Chin into chest

(Continued)

Positive Body Language	Negative Body Language
• Upright but relaxed posture	• Fidgeting
• Firm handshake	• Body sagging
• Chin up	• Self-soothe by touching oneself
• Eyebrow flash upon greeting	
• Sitting forward	

9.3 Maintaining Eye Contact

It is said that "Eyes are windows to the soul."

From Bollywood actors like Shah Rukh Khan to Hollywood stars like Denzel Washington, all are known for their magnetic onscreen performance with their eyes.

My early days at work were doing sales for a bank, DSA, where I would have to do presentations on some financial products in front of a huge crowd. I was in tears the very first day, but my team leader then just taught me one important trick—to maintain that smile and eye contact with my audience. To date, I have never looked back.

Eye contact involves seeing the audience eye-to-eye in order to establish meaningful communication. There should be a desire between the speaker and the listeners to stare into each other's eyes to enhance mutual understanding between each other.

Eye contact has been discovered to have a great influence on social behavior. Although the meanings and interpretations of eye contact can vary significantly among societies, cultures, neurotypes, and religions, it is very helpful in public speaking.

9.3.1 Benefits of Eye Contact

Figure 9.5 Importance of eye contact

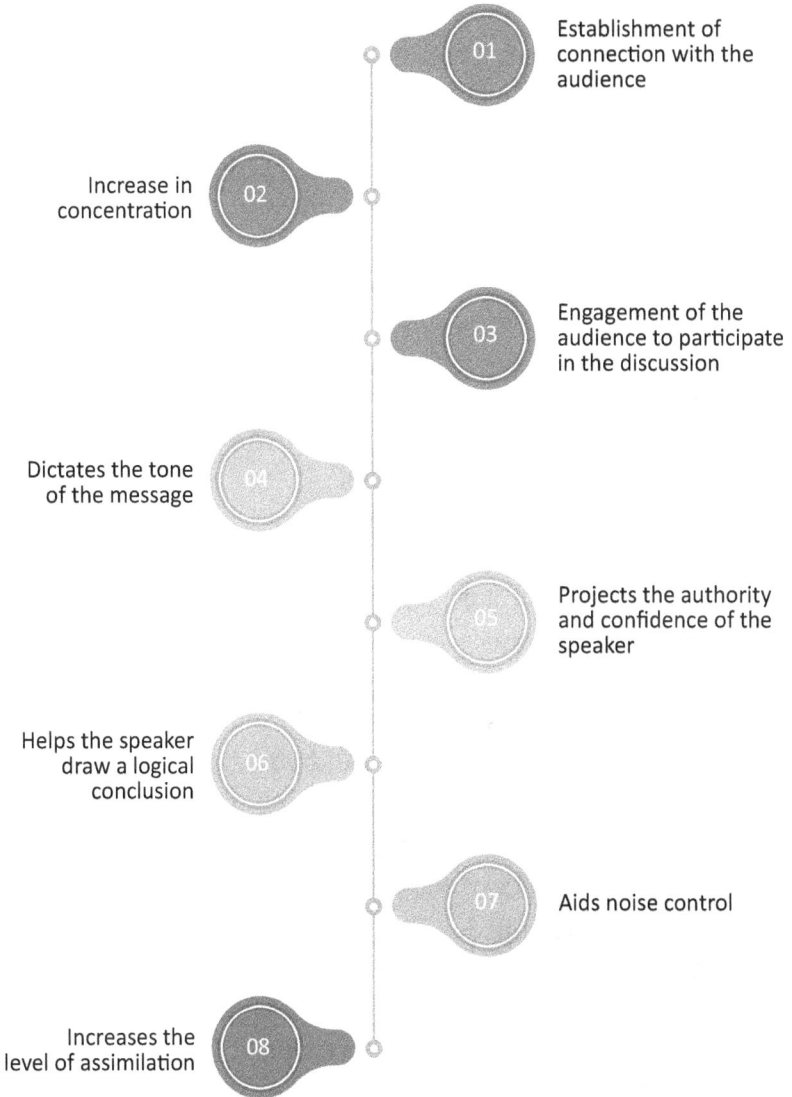

01 — Establishment of connection with the audience

02 — Increase in concentration

03 — Engagement of the audience to participate in the discussion

04 — Dictates the tone of the message

05 — Projects the authority and confidence of the speaker

06 — Helps the speaker draw a logical conclusion

07 — Aids noise control

08 — Increases the level of assimilation

Eye contact plays some significant roles in public speaking, which include but are not limited to:

1. **Establishment of connection with the audience:** A proper, good eye contact with your conversation partner or audience creates a bond of connection, which shows how concerned you are about their thoughts and needs. It also helps in building rapport.

2. **Increase in concentration:** Good eye contact allows both the speaker and the audience the opportunity to concentrate on the subject matter. It brings calmness and clears your mind from irrelevant material that can cause distraction from the essential points.

3. **Engagement of audience to participate in the discussion:** Another important advantage of eye contact is that it encourages people to participate substantially in the discussion, thereby changing passive listeners into active listeners.

4. **Dictates the tone of the message:** Psychologically, good eye contact that is accompanied by the appropriate facial expression can show the importance or tone of the message the speaker is trying to pass across. When cracking a joke, a speaker will maintain eye contact with the audience while flashing an infectious smile. This indicates a friendly tone or message.

5. **Projects the authority and confidence of the speaker:** Maintaining appropriate eye contact with an average gaze length of three to five seconds showcases the authority, courage, and confidence of the speaker during public speaking. This creates an air of authenticity and makes the audience believe the speaker's words.

6. **Helps the speaker draw a logical conclusion:** Eye contact helps speakers gauge the level of comprehension of their audience. This enables speakers to know whether or not the audience has been focusing on the message all the while before drawing their befitting, logical conclusions. When the audience looks excited and satisfied, it may indicate that the core message has sunk deep into their minds.

7. **Aids noise control:** Every eye contact you make with your listeners makes you sound more in control, confident, and powerful, leading to effective noise control in the room.

8. **Increases the level of assimilation:** The audience members pay more attention, comprehend, and remember more of what the speaker presents with frequent eye contact.

9.3.2 How to Maintain Eye Contact

Eye contact is a type of nonverbal communication that reinforces the information from speakers to their audience.

Incidentally, the meanings and interpretations of eye contact vary from one cultural background, religion, and ethnicity to another. What is a sign of respect in Western Europe may symbolize disrespect in Eastern Asian culture.

After many years of being a successful public speaker, it is my great pleasure to share with you seven tips I usually utilize in creating effective eye contact:

1. **The audience should be regarded as individual listeners:** A speaker must view their audience as individual listeners and take time to pause and scan the room for a friendly look and establish eye contact with them.

2. **Create rapport with the audience before the presentation begins:** Meeting with the audience and greeting them with a firm handshake and warm greetings will help you create good rapport and eye contact with your audience.

3. **Engage everyone in conversation:** All your audience or listeners should be carried along in your speech, and your eye contact with them can elicit a response from the audience, thereby leading to an engaging conversation with them.

4. **Eye contact must be utilized while delivering critical points:** It is very pertinent to maintain proper eye contact with your audience as you deliver vital information and critical messages in your speech.

5. **Learn to sustain eye contact for an average gaze length of three to five seconds:** A good public speaker should be able to sustain his/her eye contact long enough to make a connection. This takes an average of three to five seconds per audience member before moving on to the next person.

6. **Use the Triangle Technique (look between the eyes or at the nose of your audience):** Relax your gaze and make it appear friendly. You may begin with short bursts, which means that you should take breaks between maintaining eye contact with some members of your audience, especially those sitting in the front row.

7. **Practice with a friend (get feedback and support):** You can begin by practicing how to maintain eye contact with a friend. Ask him or her to give you honest and constructive feedback so that you can improve on how you gaze at people while delivering a speech.

9.3.3 The Relationship Between Eye Contact and Facial Expressions

A good combination of eye contact and a corresponding facial expression has proven to be a very effective tool in achieving great success in public speaking. The two techniques are important aspects of nonverbal communication, helping speakers streamline their speech delivery.

The eye contact, which is sometimes referred to as the "gateway to the soul," projects relevant index information to an audience, such as interest, attention, involvement, and disinterestedness (IAID). Factors determining these indices include length of gaze, frequency of glances, patterns of fixation, pupil dilation, and blinking rate.

In Western culture, maintaining eye contact is considered a sign of boldness, confidence, attentiveness, involvement, concentration, and honesty, while inability to maintain eye contact depicts rudeness or inattentiveness. However, cultural differences negate these ideas in Eastern Asia and Nigeria, where direct eye-gazing indicates rudeness and competitiveness, which are not socially acceptable.

As a complement, a facial expression reveals human mood and state of emotions, which may include fear, anger, surprise, contempt, disgust, happiness, and sadness. The facial expressions exhibiting these seven universally recognized emotions are the same regardless of culture, religion, or environment. However, facial expression involves the muscular control of the mouth, lips, eyes, nose, forehead, and jaw.

In public speaking, it is therefore helpful to take advantage of the complementary relationship between eye contact and facial expression to improve your presentation.

A wide pupil dilation, which is associated with attentiveness and enthusiasm, could easily be expressed as happiness when observed on a smiling face. A frequent blinking of the eye symbolizes fidgeting, fear, and lack of confidence, and this could also be noticeable by the frowning of the face and the emotion of sadness. Your audience is interestingly watching all the unspoken messages from your facial expressions.

As a public speaker, it should be noted that people smile when they are happy. Therefore, smile before you start your presentation to show the audience that you are happy, and they will smile back. A winning smile enhances eye contact. This is the first thing I do while getting on the stage as a public speaker or a trainer, and it works wonders.

9.4 Confidence Poses

Confidence poses are body postures that improve the confidence, certainty, dominance, and authority of the speaker without threatening or undermining the audience. In the same way, a confidence pose can reveal a speaker's control of affairs, openness, expansiveness, and strength.

Confidence poses, or power poses, help to build self-esteem, physical expression of confidence, assertiveness, and certainty, reducing stress and anxiety to improve one's performance in public speaking.

However, it must be handled with extreme caution to avoid being aggressive, arrogant, proud, or too complacent. They are often characterized by an upright posture, standing tall with the body taking up space and the head held high. Some examples of confidence poses include raising arms, high shoulders, spreading legs, expanding chest, posing with hands on hips, leaning forward on a table, and positioning the arms in a V-shape.

Such poses create the impression that you are confident, optimistic, strengthened, and powerful. They intend to influence the perspective of others about us and our own internal state and psyche.

9.4.1 Importance of Confidence Poses in Public Speaking

Public speaking can be overwhelming, leading to discouragement and anxiety. In order to overcome these negative emotions and improve your public speaking skills, confidence poses can be employed in various events where a display of confidence and authority is highly imperative.

The efficacy of confidence poses cannot be overemphasized as it enhances self-confidence, improves communication skills, builds performance on stage, and reduces stress and anxiety during presentations.

Two of my all-time favorite confident poses as a public speaker are the winner's V, like we have just won a match or a basketball game—and the Superman pose—with hands on your hips. Both of these poses create immense confidence in my learning.

Postures like standing straight and tall with head held high, shoulders high, broadened chest, and chin up can indicate confidence and help you breathe better, thus increasing your vocal ability. Some specific circumstances where confidence poses are very relevant include:

1. **Before Public Speaking or Presentation:** Posing confidently before embarking on an important presentation or engaging in public speaking will, to a large extent, help reduce fear and anxiety and boost self-assurance, allowing the speaker to deliver his/her message with conviction and charisma.

2. **During Social Gathering:** Confidence poses can help to showcase one's confidence and create a lasting

impression, and give room to establishing a good relationship and connection with the audience.

3.   **Job Interview or Negotiation:** A deep breath and confidence pose can increase your chances of presenting your competence and experience at job interviews.

4.   **Networking Business Events:** A confidence pose can enable you to show your expertise without prejudice when meeting new people during business networking.

5.   **Difficult Task or Competition:** Confidence poses and charisma are essentially required when facing high-pressure or stressful situations. They are very effective for maintaining composure and approaching problems with a high sense of control (see 9.6 below)

Figure 9.6 **A confident pose**

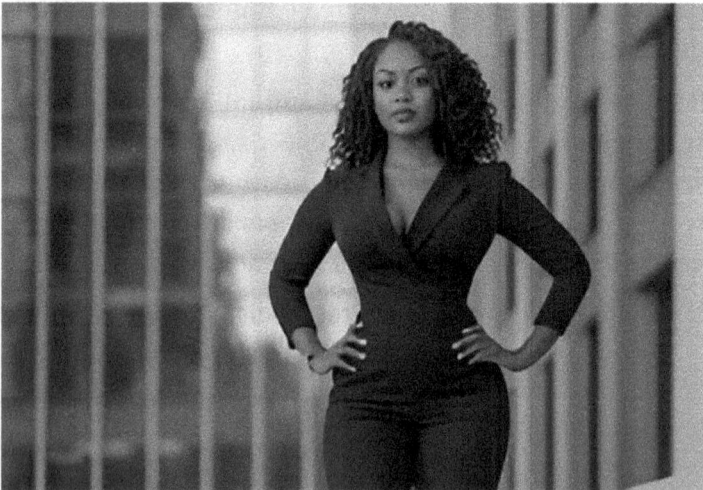

(Source: Freepik, 2025)[48]

---

48.   " A Confident Woman in A Stylish Black Outfit Poses in An Urban Setting", accessed 3 July, 2025, https://www.freepik.com/premium-ai-image/confident-woman-stylish-black-outfit-poses-urban-setting_312663940.htm

9.4.2 Effective Use of Confidence Poses

Confidence poses are essential in public speaking, but they are not the ultimate. They must be done in a clever way to avoid being misinterpreted contrary to the speaker's intention. The use of confidence poses can be effectively done by complying with the following guidelines:

1. Combine confidence poses with adequate preparation for your speaking content or material. You need to fully understand the content of your speech.

2. Display confidence poses with consideration of the tone, purpose, and expectation of your speech and your audience.

3. Practice speech presentation with confidence poses. Our message should be channeled and delivered to your audience politely.

4. Confidence poses should be chosen to reveal your intention.

5. Confidence poses can be adopted before and during speech to improve confidence and reduce stress.

6. The speaker must be respectful and empathetic and avoid offensive confidence poses that can annoy the audience.

7. A more expressive pose, such as gesturing, pointing, or moving around the stage with a fascinating smile and nodding, can be used to reinforce your message and connect with your audience on a personal level.

Chapter Summary

- Nonverbal communication is very important for public speakers in the sense that they can use body language, gestures, and eye contact, which are different types of nonverbal communication, to complement their verbal delivery.

- Depending on their meanings, interpretations, and applications (as guided by different religions, cultures, ethnicities, etc.), public speakers can enhance their audience's understanding by utilizing body language and gestures that they understand.

- To be effective, gestures must be properly utilized. Speakers should refrain from using gestures that may be offensive to their audience.

- Maintaining sensible eye contact while delivering their speeches may help public speakers connect deeply with their audience. Prolonged or probing eye contact may be repulsive and culturally inappropriate in some cultures. So, speakers should do their homework by learning about the cultural sensibilities of their audience before appearing in their presence.

- Confidence poses give speakers the opportunity to appear confident and in control of their presentations while standing in front of their audience. However, speakers should avoid using power poses that may be wrongly considered as proud and condescending by their audience.

Quiz

1. Nonverbal communication entails using one's body language and gestures to communicate certain messages to an audience.
   a. True
   b. False

2. Which of these is NOT considered a kind of nonverbal communication?
   a. Facial expression
   b. Gestures
   c. Spoken words

3. The following are advantages of utilizing gestures except for _____ .
   a. Attracting attention
   b. Expressing emotions
   c. Confusing the audience

4. Nonverbal communication can engender better interpersonal relationships and foster understanding between the audience and the speaker.
   a. False
   b. True

5. How many types of gestures are there?
   a. 6
   b. 7
   c. 10

6. _____ is a type of gesture that involves touching behaviors and movement to show how you feel internally, which may involve arousal or anxiety.

   a. Emblems

   b. Adaptors

   c. Illustrators

7. The kind of gestures used to represent abstract concepts is called _____ .

   a. Adaptors

   b. Metaphoric gestures

   c. Illustrators

8. The kind of gestures that follow the rhythm, pacing, and cadence of a speaker's speech but do not necessarily describe the speech content are known as _____

   a. Illustrators

   b. Emblems

   c. Beat gestures

9. When people cover their mouths when they are amazed or shocked is an example of _____

   a. Iconic gestures

   b. Manipulator gestures

   c. Deictic gestures

10. What does the gesture shaking your head side-to-side mean?

    a. Saying yes

    b. Saying no

    c. Saying maybe

Answer Key

1 – a	2 – c	3 – c	4 – b	5 – b
6 – b	7 – b	8 – c	9 – b	10 – b

CHAPTER 10

Creating Interactive Presentations

Key Learning Objectives

- Explore techniques for audience engagement
- Understand how to handle questions and feedback
- Learning how to encourage participation

Imagine walking into a kitchen. The aromas of sizzling spices fill the air; you carefully choose your ingredients and, with practiced skills, craft a dish that delights the senses. A good presentation is no different—it's an artful blend of preparation, delivery, and engagement, designed to leave a lasting impression on the audience.

Much like a well-cooked meal, a great presentation requires thought, balance, and execution. Too much information overwhelms, and too little leaves the audience unsatisfied. The secret lies in choosing the right ingredients, adding the perfect seasoning, and serving it in a way that captivates and satisfies.

In this chapter, we will explore how to craft presentations that inform, engage, and inspire.

10.1 Techniques for Audience Engagement

The concept of characterizing or knowing one's audience pretty well comes into play in this scenario. Before any public speaker can effectively engage with their audience, they must know their audience's demographics, knowledge levels, psychographics, purpose of attendance, etc.

10.1.1 VIBES PQ – 7 Proven Techniques That Instantly Engage Any Audience

Have you ever been in a room with an engaging speaker who made time fly while enthralling the audience throughout?

It wasn't because of their message, but how they delivered it!

After 20 years of working in communication and training as a public speaker, I've discovered that these 7 core techniques consistently separate an *average* speaker from an *engaging one*. These techniques work across cultures, industries, and audiences—whether you're addressing a boardroom, a classroom, or a crowd of thousands.

To help you remember them, I've put them into one simple acronym: VIBES PQ

Let's carefully explore why these 7 elements matter so much—and how they can transform your speaking career:

V – Vocal Variety

You should understand that your voice is more than sound—it's a vehicle for your *emotions*. By varying your volume, pace, tone, and pitch, you can indicate transitions, emphasize key points, and prevent your speech from being boring. A flat tone can cause you to lose your audience's attention fast; variety will keep them curious and alert.

Why it works: Vocal variety is believed to stimulate different parts of the brain. And this will keep your audience neurologically engaged.

I – Intentional Body Language

Your actions or body language speak loudly, even when you are silent.

Pay attention to your facial expressions, open gestures, and posture. When you move purposefully, you convey clarity, confidence, and warmth.

Why it works: 55% of communication is nonverbal. When you align your body language with your core message, it builds trust through the reinforcement of your spoken words.

B – Being a Listener

To become an engaging speaker, you need to listen more than you speak.

Watch your audience's facial reactions, respond accordingly to their body language cues, and even consider their real-time feedback. This two-way approach will surely build a genuine connection.

Why it works: When an audience feels appreciated, they become very friendly and feel connected with the speaker.

E – Effective Pauses

Consider silence as your superpower. By strategically pausing during speeches, you can let your words sink in, invoke some drama, and give your audience time to reflect and react.

Why it works: Normally, pauses generate anticipation, calm the audience's nerves, and add more weight to the speaker's message.

S – Storytelling

Facts may show your audience the level of your expertise, but it is your story that will sell your core ideas.

Human beings are naturally wired for captivating stories—they engage our emotions, spark fresh imaginations, and make a speaker's message unforgettable to us. A good story can reveal more vital information than 10 slides can.

Why it works: Stories naturally activate our brain's sensory cortex, making it possible for us to remember 22x more than data alone.

P – Powerful Eye Contact

Great speakers communicate with their eyes, not just with their mouths. When you look keenly into someone's eyes, you build a personal connection—even in a group. This gesture shows control, sincerity, and attentiveness.

Why it works: By default, eye contact helps you build rapport immediately with your listeners.

Q – Questioning Techniques

Asking your audience pertinent questions is the best way to actively involve them in the speech.

Whether they are rhetorical or interactive, sensible questions will nudge your audience to reflect, hold dialogues with each other, and *feel included* in your message.

Why it works: Pertinent questions will activate the prefrontal cortex, which usually prompts critical thinking and emotional connection.

Bringing It All Together

When you utilize **VIBES PQ**, your audience will find you to be:

- More understandable
- More memorable
- More dependable

10.2 Handling Questions and Feedback

It is one of the best practices in public speaking, if time permits, to often allow some members of the audience to ask some sensible questions. By following the essential steps, the question-and-feedback sessions can be successfully handled:

1. **Preparing for Questions:** Experienced speakers don't usually wait until the end of their speeches to know what kind of questions the audience may throw at them. They actually anticipate some questions related to the topics of their speeches and properly prepare answers for them. As a speaker, put yourself in the position of your audience for a second: What kind of questions are you likely to ask any speaker who will talk about the topic you are delivering? You can make a list of three to four questions and then provide appropriate responses to them.

Before going in for your presentation, you should decide whether the audience will be allowed to ask questions at the beginning, middle, or end of your speech.

2.   **During the Presentation:** One common mistake new speakers make during the question-and-feedback sessions is not listening actively or paying full attention to the questions being asked before attempting to answer them.

When you listen attentively to an audience member before jumping into answering it, this demonstrates that you are showing due respect to the questioner and have fully understood his/her question(s).

In certain circumstances, you may find it difficult to completely understand the questions being asked. In those situations, do not assume you know everything; repeat or paraphrase the question to confirm it with the questioner and let the others hear it before deciding to answer it.

Even for experienced speakers, standing in front of an audience can be nerve-wracking. Stay calm or be composed, even if you are asked a challenging question. Be honest when attempting to answer the question. Let your answer(s) be concise and relevant to the questions. If you are struggling with providing an appropriate answer, admit that you don't know the answer. You may offer to follow up with the one who asked the question later.

3.   **After the Presentation:** Don't be that shy speaker who tries to avoid post-presentation questions at all costs. Instead, you should intentionally invite feedback and

questions from your audience to demonstrate openness and willingness to help them to the best of your ability.

For clarity, you may need to separate constructive feedback from unwarranted, negative criticism. When providing your answers, concentrate mainly on practical points. It is advisable to show appreciation to your audience members for their questions and feedback, whether it is positive or negative.

Sometimes, time may not permit you to answer all their questions; promise the audience that you will follow up with them with an email or a newsletter where you will properly address all the unanswered questions.

4. **Handling Negative Questions and Feedback:** Speakers are advised to be professional all the time because sometimes rude, irrelevant, and inappropriate questions might be thrown at them while delivering a speech. In such circumstances, respond calmly and refrain from becoming overtly defensive.

You should endeavor to understand the questioners' perspectives and their underlying concerns. Acknowledge the fact that you know how they feel about the subject matter and offer sensible and well-structured responses to prove your points.

| Figure 10.1 | Guide to handling questions during the speech |

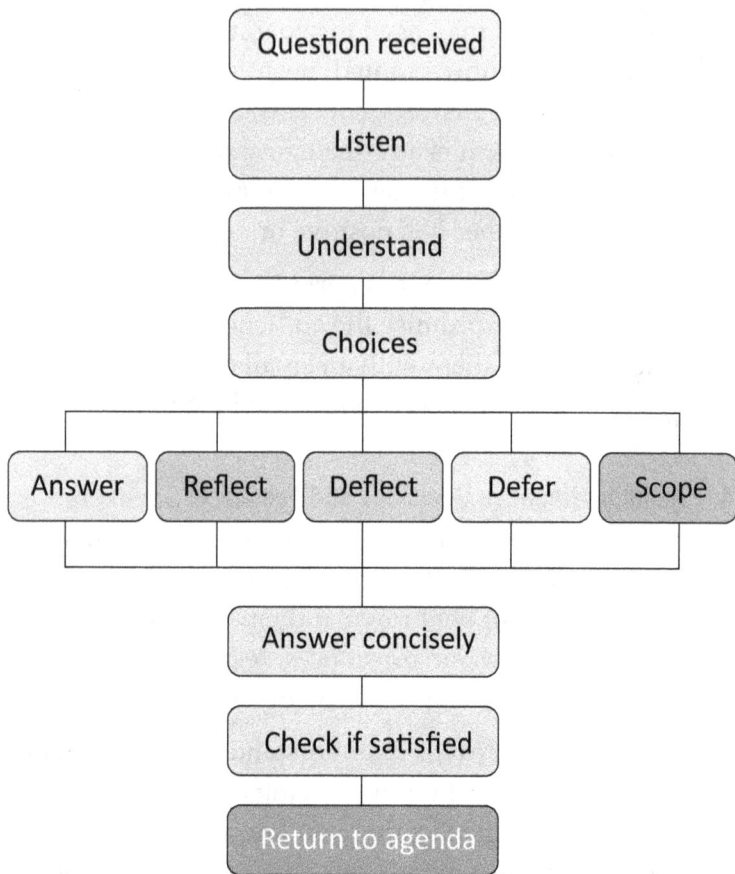

```
┌─────────────────────────┐
│    Question received     │
└─────────────────────────┘
             │
┌─────────────────────────┐
│         Listen           │
└─────────────────────────┘
             │
┌─────────────────────────┐
│       Understand         │
└─────────────────────────┘
             │
┌─────────────────────────┐
│        Choices           │
└─────────────────────────┘
             │
  ┌──────┬──────┬──────┬──────┬──────┐
┌──────┐┌──────┐┌───────┐┌──────┐┌──────┐
│Answer││Reflect││Deflect││ Defer││Scope │
└──────┘└──────┘└───────┘└──────┘└──────┘
  └──────┴──────┴──────┴──────┴──────┘
             │
┌─────────────────────────┐
│     Answer concisely     │
└─────────────────────────┘
             │
┌─────────────────────────┐
│     Check if satisfied   │
└─────────────────────────┘
             │
┌─────────────────────────┐
│     Return to agenda     │
└─────────────────────────┘
```

(Adapted from Virtualspeech.com, 2017)[49]

10.3 Encouraging Participation

Great speeches require the active participation of both the speakers and their audiences. In other words, a speaker will end up talking to himself or herself if his/her audience isn't

---

49. "Guide for Handling Questions after a Presentation", http://Virtualspeech.com, accessed 4 July, 2025, https://virtualspeech.com/blog/guide-for-handling-questions-after-a-presentation

responding to or participating in the entire speech-delivery process.

Figure 10.2   **Benefits of encouraging participation**

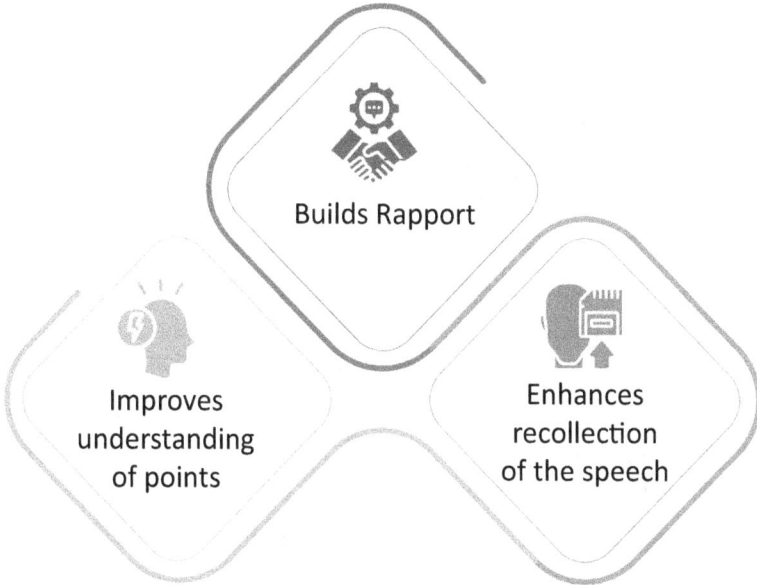

(Source: Omind, 2024)[50]

Highlighted below are some of the well-known approaches any speaker can adopt in encouraging more participation from his/her audience:

1. **Asking rhetorical questions:** By asking rhetorical questions, a speaker can get his/her audience into a participatory mode without necessarily prodding them to provide immediate answers to the questions asked. You may pose questions that will cause your audience to take some actions, such as raising their

---

50. "10 Audience Engagement Strategies That Work", Omind, accessed 7 July, 2025, https://www.omind.ai/blogs/audience-engagement-strategies

hands, standing up on their feet, or undertaking some nonverbal actions like stretching or exercising. Standing polling is also a great technique; you can say, *"How many of you agree with my statement? If you do, please stand to your feet!"*

2. **Using polls and surveys:** Undertaking real-time surveying or polling can increase audience participation. There are some apps or devices designed to connect people who are currently attending the same conferences, seminars, or workshops to socialize. Using pre-event surveys can help a speaker to know how to tailor his/her speech in accordance with the audience's needs.

3. **Incorporating interactive elements:** Speakers are usually advised to utilize live demos or group activities that can encourage their audience to be actively involved in their speech delivery. The audience can be divided into small groups of panelists discussing certain aspects of the speech or engaging in group activities.

4. **Using humor:** Light-hearted or well-timed jokes can be used to make the audience comfortable with the speaker. Some interactive humor can require that the audience participate in funny skits or improvised activities.

5. **Offering incentives:** Public speakers can increase their audience participation by offering prizes and rewards to active members. These small incentives can include, but are not limited to, gift cards or other freebies. By recognizing active audience members with thank-you notes, public appreciation, or social media shoutouts, speakers can motivate their audience to be fully committed to their speech delivery.

6. **Using technology:** While delivering their speeches, public speakers can use apps that permit real-time interaction among attendees, like live voting, commenting, or Q&A applications. The advancement in virtual reality is giving people the opportunity to enjoy immersive experiences, whereby someone can attend and contribute to a conference proceeding while living thousands of kilometers away from the actual conference venue.

There are also some online platforms, social media, or event apps where the audience can post questions or comments related to the conference they are currently attending.

Chapter Summary

- A public speaker can employ effective techniques of vocal variety, body language, storytelling, effective use of pauses, eye contact, and audience interaction to proactively engage their audience.

- A professional speaker understands that he/she must handle questions thrown at him/her by the audience calmly, cohesively, and convincingly.

- It is not every time that the audience behaves appropriately. For instance, addressing a group of unionists or community activists may draw some negative feedback. In this situation, a professional speaker is still expected to be cool-headed and well-composed, providing pertinent responses to harsh criticism. Sometimes, it may be sensible to offer a post-presentation follow-up to clear the air about any misunderstood points.

- Public speaking is about genuine and mutually beneficial interaction between speakers and their audience. Therefore, it is imperative that speakers employ different tactics to encourage their audience to actively participate in the presentation or event.

Quiz

1. Knowing their audience's demographics, knowledge levels, psychographics, purpose of attendance, etc., can help public speakers engage actively with their audience.

   a. False
   b. True

2. Experienced public speakers understand that they need to use different tones, speaking speeds, and pitches to keep their audience interested in the messages being delivered to them.

   a. True
   b. False

3. One noticeable benefit of adopting vocal variety for public speakers is that they can _____

   a. Use a fake accent to deceive their audience
   b. Emphasize key points and appropriately rouse their audience's emotions
   c. Pretend to be a great speaker to their audience

4. Body language is a visual tool speakers can use to deeply connect with their audience. Which of these is NOT usually regarded as body language?

   a. A gesture
   b. A facial expression
   c. Tone of voice

5. **It is very important for public speakers to pay attention to cultural sensibilities when using eye contact to connect with their audience.**

   a. True
   b. False

6. **In Japan, China, or South Korea, what is considered an acceptable eye-contact practice?**

   a. Staring into someone's eyes for a very long time.
   b. Looking away when speaking with an elderly person.
   c. A prolonged gaze into the eyes of someone who is of the opposite gender/sex.

7. **However, in the Western world, maintaining a firm eye contact indicates _____**

   a. Dishonesty
   b. Shyness
   c. Showing interest in someone or something

8. **How useful is pausing to speakers while delivering their speeches?**

   a. It allows their audience to absorb some vital information
   b. It gives the speakers a long time to rest
   c. Pausing between speeches is not useful to speakers

9. How should a mature speaker handle a heckler while talking to an audience?

   a. The speaker should get angry and fight with the heckler
   b. The speaker should be composed, calm, and offer coherent responses
   c. The speaker should just ignore the heckler

10. The best approach for speakers to prepare for questions asked during their speech delivery is to anticipate them by putting themselves in the position of the audience.

    a. False
    b. True

Answer Key

1 – b	2 – a	3 – b	4 – c	5 – a
6 – b	7 – c	8 – a	9 – b	10 – b

CHAPTER 11

Adapting to Different Settings

Key Learning Objectives

- Understanding the difference in speaking in small meetings vs. large conferences vs panel discussions
- Exploring virtual presentations and webinars
- Learning strategies for different professional contexts and standing out

As far as communication is concerned, public speaking is one of the best ways to communicate, inspire, and persuade people. But being a great speaker is more than just preparing and delivering a good speech; it is also being able to adjust and respond to different events' needs. Whether you are addressing a close company gathering, speaking to a full-swing convention center, or motivating a sea of fans in an open space, the location greatly affects the understanding of the message. This skill also allows you to have an improved experience with the audience and guarantees that your message will always carry the same level of meaning.

Here is an applicable quote I created about adaptability for speakers: "True communication power lies in the ability to adapt—whether addressing a stadium, a Zoom room, or a single listener over coffee."

11.1 Speaking in Small Meetings vs Large Conferences vs Panel Discussions

The required dynamics for speaking in small meetings, large conferences, or participation in panel discussions are distinctly different. In these situations, speakers must adapt their communication strategies, including how they present their speech, the tone of voice, and the kinds of engaging techniques they utilize while speaking. Such adaptability helps not only in effective communication but also assists speakers in earning trust and building good relations with their audience.

Figure 11.1 Large groups vs Small groups

Large Group	Small Group
Audience-oriented	Interpersonal
High inspiration	Deep support
Anonymity	Intimacy
Acquaintances	Deep relationships
Expectation	Discussion
Generating new small groups	Providing a safe place

(Adapted from Kelly Montgomery, 2025)[51]

51. "Large Group, Small Group, Inspiration, Deep Support, Anonymity, Intimacy, Acquaintances, Deep Relationships, Expectation, and Discussion", Kelly Montgomery, accessed 5 July, 2025, https://slideplayer.com/slide/6635711/

11.1.1 Speaking in Small Meetings

Anytime you are speaking at small meetings, you will likely feel some sort of personal and tactile interaction with the audience. Bigger settings encourage open discussions and more participation, so speakers can talk to their audience better since the audience is in closer proximity. As John C. Maxwell remarked, *"People don't care how much you know until they know how much you care."* Small meetings offer people or attendees the rare and always cherished opportunity to connect on a deeper level. In other words, in a small group, participants can mingle freely and informally exchange pleasantries, including knowing one another by name.

The apparent key features of small gatherings include achieving relevance, quick responsiveness, and clarity. In this scenario, speakers can maintain good eye contact with a small number of attendees and engage in active listening to instantly gauge their reactions to their speeches or topics under discussion. Small groups make it possible for speakers to request real-time comments or feedback and, using a conversational tone, provide helpful responses that will keep the attendees engagingly motivated.

Sometimes, personal anecdotes or specific examples will help to create that connection and trust, and have a positive effect here.

Speaking in small groups is quite different from speaking to large audiences because it entails a different mindset. For small group discussions, everyone's voice is important, and as a speaker, you must give support to the discussion and speak. Because of such close interactions, there is the natural cultivation of respect, participation, and creativity, which makes small meetings an ideal environment for the exchange of ideas and effective working in teams and relationships.

11.1.2 Commanding the Stage: Public Speaking at Large Conferences

Addressing a large gathering is a priceless experience, but at the same time, it is a tough thing to do, as it calls for thorough planning, an air of charm, and some level of spontaneity. It is an opportunity to market your experience, reach out to many people, and advance your career in a wider sphere. But admittedly, being up in front of a big crowd also has its bittersweet upside, as it can be fun, but it can also be very scary.

It is Dale Carnegie who is quoted as saying, *"The only way to get over your stage fright is to get up and speak."* Such statements do inspire confidence and are a good motivator, but earning that confidence and utilizing it is the first challenge that the individual must overcome. The stage is set for success when the wheels are set in motion, or rather, the preparations are done. A serious debate touches on the topic of thoroughly rehearsing. As one presents their argument, they practice their punchlines, plan for any possible problems, and adjust to the event's atmosphere. When speaking to a large audience, direct communication is a must. Initiating with a problem and responding with a story or question, and summarizing with a call to action are all crucial elements of a successful presentation.

In contrast to smaller gatherings where everyone's voice is heard, a conference requires that one projects both their voice and personality to occupy space in the room. Intimidating gestures, having a loud speaking voice, and dramatic pauses can capture the attention of the audience. The use of slides and video clips can be used to back the arguments and enhance the audience's enjoyment. In this circumstance, the use of a narrative is crucial. A well-told story can create a shared sense of reality for diverse audiences.

At the end of the day, the entire task of addressing a large audience is meant to impress on every member an experience that they went through together. With diligent practice and determination, one can dispel the negativity completely and render the occasion memorable to all.[52]

11.1.3 Panel Discussions: Navigating the Conversation

Panel discussions are distinct; they're both a platform for individual expression and a shared conversation. It is a collaborative discussion while giving a keynote address, where all the focus is on you. This kind of deep listening is crucial on a panel because it determines how well you perform with the moderator as well as other panelists.

There are group dynamics that include issues such as sharing time when speaking, engaging with other speakers while on the same podium, and answering questions from the audience. Consequently, do your homework. Know the issues intimately, which questions you expect to be asked, and the answers that other panel guests are likely to give. This helps ensure that your input is meaningful in a way that it does not replicate or conflict with other inputs. Since time is generally short, it is important to make your remarks brief and on point to keep the audience engaged.

In principle, great panelists tend to show some degree of flexibility when deliberating on their discussion topics. Instead of controlling the direction of the conversations, they let contributors suggest how the discussions will progress, striking a neutral stance most of the time. A

---

52. Grace Lancaster, *Public Speaking with Confidence: Conquer Anxiety, Captivate any Audience, and Harness Technology to Crush Your Presentation* (Amazon, 2024),, 45-80.

panelist's overarching responsibility is to keep the discourse civil, ensuring every participant is respectful, considerate, and thoughtful in their contributions. On other occasions, panelists may streamline the process by providing humorous but relevant stories, examples, and analogies that panel contributors can utilize to further expand their points. The accomplishment of this format of a panel discussion is not only improving one's professional competencies but also furthering the social discourse and imparting the audience with beneficial knowledge that they had not had prior.

11.2 Virtual Presentations and Webinars

In the present digital era, virtual presentations and webinars have become almost necessary forms of interaction, as they offer unparalleled ease of access and use. From internal office groups to global audiences and web conferences, connecting with people authentically requires a varied skill set. In contrast to live events, online webinars offer no physical cues; thus, participants tend to disengage from the conversations.

11.2.1 Virtual Presentations: Learning the Art of Remote Communication

Due to their apparent ease of use and access, webinars and virtual presentations are widely utilized by modern public speakers. However, the main challenges for adopting these tools include, but are not limited to, the audience having difficulty in maintaining focus over a long period of time, the possibility of disconnection owing to technical issues, and speakers' inability to truly gauge their audience's genuine feelings. To sensibly resolve these problems, efforts are required on the part of the public speakers, and the following steps are recommended to decisively deal with these challenges:

1. **Optimizing technology setup:** Purchase a good webcam and microphone, and ensure that your internet connection is reliable because a bad internet connection will affect your voice and delivery. Troubleshoot the setup to ensure that all technological devices are functioning properly. Doing this, you will be able to identify any technical glitches before your virtual presentations or webinars begin. You may also need to familiarize yourself with other communication platforms, such as Google Meet and Zoom, and master how to share screens, transform backgrounds, and chat with members of your audience.

2. **Designing visually appealing content:** In this digital age, visuals play a significant role in helping the online audience grasp the core messages being delivered by public speakers virtually, since they cannot derive adequate, meaningful cues from speakers' body language or facial appearances. As a speaker, it is important that you professionally prepare clean slides that have a few texts but are rich in self-explanatory graphics. It will also be helpful and engaging for your audience if you can incorporate some infographics, videos, and animations in your slides. To accomplish some of these tasks, you may need to use some virtual tools such as Concept Board, Miro, or Mentimeter.

3. **Refining your unique delivery style:** It is advisable that you refine the delivery of your online presentations to constantly keep your audience engaged. This may require using voice modulation effects to convey your core messages to them. Cultivate the habit of looking eye-to-eye or maintaining eye contact with your

audience by looking straight into the camera. Smile often and offer some visible, understandable facial gestures/expressions to intentionally entertain and carry your listeners along.

4. **Engaging your audience:** Speakers can keep their virtual audience engaged in many ways. One of the best practices is to actively involve your audience in thoughtful activities such as participating in polls, Q&As, and chats, and providing solutions to quizzes and puzzles, all of which can be done while online. It is equally important to create an inclusive environment, making everyone feel welcomed and appreciated.

5. **Mastering time management:** The main downside of online meetings is how to sustain the audience's focus or concentration, owing to their short attention span. It has been proven that structuring one's speech into short sections and utilizing flawless transitions can help the audience stay glued to a speaker's presentation. It is also advisable to use as many visual cues as necessary to proactively keep the audience entertained and motivated. For long online presentations, allowing the attendees to have short breaks in between sections can practically eliminate boredom.

6. **Creating a distraction-free environment:** It is important to ensure that there is no noise, clutter, or a person (any family member or friend) in your background while holding online training sessions or meetings; otherwise, your audience will be distracted. If you are using a virtual background, make sure it is plain, simple, and related to your presentation theme—avoid using a background containing weird graphics that can divert your audience's attention from the main business.

7. **Preparing for technological challenges:** As a speaker, always put in place a backup plan that will quickly address any technical challenges that may arise while delivering your online speeches. More often than not, technical problems occur without any prior warning, and this may affect the quality of your presentations. When this happens, don't panic at all. Keep your audience in the loop by emailing or calling them to explain what the problem is, and as a professional, you should quickly resolve the technical issues.

8. **Following up after the presentation:** Professional speakers understand that the right thing to do after an online presentation is to stay in touch with their audience for a couple of reasons. First, to reinforce whatever they might have learned during the presentation by sharing recorded audio or videos of the online sessions, providing additional materials or resources that they can access, and sending them an email summary of the entire presentation. Second, to reach out to the audience for constructive feedback.

Figure 11.2	The day of the event

Preparation for virtual meetings!

Backup plans:

This includes having a backup microphone, a strong wifi connection or data, as well as keeping all the devices sufficiently charged in case the electricity goes off.

Stage setup:

This includes the lighting, the sound system, and the background visuals. Make sure your background is clear of any distracting elements.

Introductory and closing remarks:

It is important to ensure that the introduction and closing remarks are accurate and aligned with the speaker's message.

(Adapted from SpeakersU, 2025)[53]

11.2.2 Webinars: How to Connect to Remote Audiences with Accuracy and Interactivity

Webinars incorporate formalized and purposeful communication with audiences through content-rich interactions virtually. That is unlike virtual meetings, where there is more interaction and collaboration, which makes webinars quite remote; participating in a seminar typically involves listening to a presenter who addresses a wider range

---

53. "Keynote Speaker Pre-Event Checklist: A Comprehensive Guide for Corporate Meeting and Conference Organizers.", SpeakersU, accessed 7 July, 2025, https://speakersu.com/guides/keynote-speaker-pre-event-checklist/

of people. They require a careful fusion of teaching, audience engagement, and sheer fun, thus making it a distinct type of public address.

Understanding the characteristics of the webinar is vital for its successful implementation. Thus, it is crucial to balance the preparation of the event with ensuring engagement of participants for the purpose of targeting the audience and the effectiveness of the message.

11.2.3 Difference between virtual meetings and webinars

Even though webinars and virtual meetings both utilize remote communication, they have distinct features that are peculiar to each of them.

1. **Audience Size:** Webinars normally target bigger crowds through the use of a one-to-many communication style. On the other hand, virtual meetings can be large gatherings with an emphasis on conversations among the participants.

2. **Purpose:** A webinar aims to disseminate information, primarily using content such as a presentation, a training, or a demonstration. Whereas for virtual meetings, the purpose is more for presentations or collaboration, where the discussions and decisions are made.

3. **Interactivity:** Questions on online presentations make the attendees understand that attention is not scattered among multiple speakers but rather focused on the one who gives the presentation. However, in a virtual meeting, everyone is given a chance to speak in the discussion.

Speaking in a webinar can turn into an engaging presentation for an audience who is not physically present. They differ from virtual meetings, where they are more planned and led by a presenter who must make sure that the content that is provided is useful and the attention of the target audience is not lost. For the webinars to bear fruit, the speakers should direct their efforts towards content, technology, and appearance. In this manner, the audience will be well educated, well-motivated, and thirsty for more knowledge.

11.3 Strategies for Different Professional Contexts and Standing Out

As a public speaker, one must progress and stand out in a new professional environment, and this requires a well-thought-out and organized plan as well as practice on the specifics of the audience response. This section explores how a public speaker's performance can be improved in numerous verticals and positions an individual as an effective communicator.

11.3.1 Strategies for Different Professional Contexts

1. **Corporate Presentations:** A corporate presentation has a strict framework that is accuracy-oriented, formal-language-oriented, and presents information in data form. Storytelling expert Nancy Duarte, in her book "Resonate," explains how an audience is not interested in a non-structured presentation.[54] Presentation aids like tables and diagrams also serve to emphasize the salient points of a discussion that is prepared via a practice session. One must get it right. Use terms of the

---

54. Nancy Duarte. *Resonate: Present Visual Stories that Transform Audiences* (John Wiley and Sons, 2010) 57.

trade only when needed, but avoid too much jargon. An audience respects a speaker with a calm voice and a firm stance. It builds confidence in the audience.

2. **Education and Training Sessions:** The most important aspects of the educational and training sessions are clarity, simplicity, and interactivity. Jason Silva emphasizes that learning through stories gets rid of the barriers framing complex ideas.[55] One can use unique real-life situations, metaphors, and pertinent questions to explain more difficult issues. Audience analysis should be the first step in the process of engaging the audience and ensuring that every aspect of the presentation is appropriate for the audience.

3. **Inspirational and Motivational Speeches:** When a speaker addresses their audience, there must be a strong emotional appeal and personal relevance. As Tony Robbins puts it, *"It is all about storytelling."* For example, sharing a person's hardship and how he/she overcame those challenges is a message that can easily be absorbed by the receivers and can also be deeply felt. Zero-to-hero stories work very well with the audience. The whole thing is finding the correct level of passion so that the audience is inspired rather than being preached at.

4. **Conference Keynotes:** A keynote address is the best way to influence the tone of an event, such as a conference. It's worth noting that Simon Sinek, in his Start with Why TED Talk[56], expands on Tad's point about starting

---

55. Jason Silva, "Jason Silva's Origin Story | Origins: The Journey of Humankind", YouTube, 2:29,. https://www.youtube.com/watch?v=peXVGSGllvo

56. Simon Sinek, "Start with why -- How Great Leaders Inspire Action | Simon Sinek TEDxPugetSound". Microsoft Bing.https://www.bing.com/videos/riverview/relatedvideo?q=noting+that+Simon+Sinek%2c+in+his+Start+with+Why+TED+Talk&mid=98A8E88B256F2759A00298A8E88B256F2759A002&FORM=VIRE

with an attention-grabbing idea or question. To effect the desired change, you must first analyze the event's theme, study the audience, and tailor your speech to the conference's objectives in a way that is consistent with the conference's objectives. A good start, an energetic presence on stage, and a motivating message are all required for an impactful presentation.

A powerful presentation can start with an alarming statistic. If you are delivering a speech against smoking, you can say, "*There are about **8 million premature deaths** worldwide every year. Approximately more than **7 million** result from direct tobacco use, while an additional **1.3 million** are caused by exposure to second-hand smoke.*"

You can equally begin with an emotional personal story to immediately hook the attention of your audience. If you are addressing a team of accountants, you can say, "*My friends started calling me a magician when I was in primary school. Why? Because I was good with numbers then, even now. Before they could finish asking me any mathematical questions, I would tell them the correct answers right there! So, they thought I was a magician with numbers!*"

11.3.2 Standing out as a seasoned public speaker.

1. **Have a Distinct Voice:** It is worth noting that most great public speakers have a distinct style that is unique to each of them, which easily appeals to their audience. For example, it's said that Les Brown has some of the most inspiring, relatable, and striking messages. Whatever the case, if the edge is comedic, motivational, or authoritative, then possessing a trademark voice will

aid in making an impact and reaching the most distant audiences.

2. **Embrace Continuous Learning and Adaptation:** A public speaker cannot remain stagnant; instead, they must constantly grow. Learning new styles of communication, adapting to new technologies, and following up on feedback are just a few of them. Famous orator Brian Tracy recommends these practices to aid a speaker's ability to enhance his or her performance through persistence.[57] We live in complicated times, and being flexible in your approach allows you to be able to provide for a wide range of audiences and situations.

3. **Foster Bonds and Offer Your True Self:** Without doubt, the primary element in a great communicator is authenticity. Brené Brown says that relatability, vulnerability, and the strength of a story are what a speaker should focus on.[58] Trust is developed when you are real, and in return, you have a bond with your audience that makes your message valuable and unforgettable.

4. **Perfect the Art of Nonverbal Communication:** Ignoring your body language, facial expressions, and gestures can be the same as ignoring what you are saying. Nonverbal cues, posture, and eye contact can assist in communicating a great deal, states social psychologist Amy Cuddy.[59] All these small things can ensure that an

---

57. "10 Tips for Improving Your Public Speaking Skills", *Harvard Professional & Executive Development, accessed 5 June, 2025.* https://professional.dce.harvard.edu/blog/10-tips-for-improving-your-public-speaking-skills/

58. Brene Brown. "The Power of Vulnerability", *TED*, accessed 8 July, 2025, https://www.ted.com/talks/brene_brown_the_power_of_vulnerability

59. "Body Language and Nonverbal Communication: Communicating Without Words", HelpGuide.org, accessed 2 July, 2025, https://www.helpguide.org/relationships/communication/nonverbal-communication

audience's focus is on what you have to say rather than other distractions.

5. **Leverage Technology and Media:** With technology at our disposal, we readily have the potential to bring the presentation to a richer and more captivating multi-media dimension, which is what experienced speakers know how to do. A good instance of this would be Steve Jobs of Apple, who was particularly noted for his launches, where visuals and specific pacing with voice and story were expertly handled. In other words, the use of such tools and engaging techniques makes the information presentation an interactive one, thus enabling the audience to have a memorable experience rather than having reasoning work against the technology employed.

Chapter summary

- There are stark differences in speaking at different venues, such as in small meetings, large conferences, or participating in panel discussions.

- While speakers need to prepare well before appearing at any of these venues, most public speakers find participating in panel discussions to be the least strenuous, closely followed by speaking to a few people in small meetings. Large conferences are the most strenuous for public speakers, and new speakers may fumble in front of a large audience if they have not prepared enough for it.

- A large percentage of virtual presentations and webinars occur online, and what separates these two online presentation formats is that virtual presentations can have a smaller audience than webinars. In virtual meetings, the audience has a better chance of actively contributing to the discussion, unlike a webinar. In a webinar, the subject of discussion may be about a particular topic or theme; however, virtual presentations may cover more topics than webinars.

- Some of the strategies that speakers can adopt for different professional contexts and standing out among the pack include, but are not limited to, having a distinct voice, having a deep knowledge of the topic, being inspirational/ motivating, understanding the use of multimedia and some communication technologies, etc.

Quiz

1. Which of these speaking venues stresses most public speakers?

   a. Panels
   b. Small meetings
   c. Large conferences

2. To stand out from the crowd, public speakers must master some aspects of nonverbal communication.

   a. True
   b. False

3. While speaking in small meetings, speakers are often encouraged to feel personally connected with their audience, to the point of even touching some of the audience members.

   a. False
   b. True

4. When comparing large conferences with small meetings, which of these is not possible for a speaker addressing a larger audience?

   a. Ability to relate personally with some members of the audience
   b. Making the speech audience-centered
   c. Encouraging more participation from the audience

5. To become a successful panelist, one must be prepared, flexible, time-conscious, and considerate of other panelists.
    a. False
    b. True

6. It is a fact that not all speakers are suitable for delivering virtual presentations. In order to be good at virtual presentations, a speaker must _____
    a. Disregard the presentation context and speak only on his/her personal experiences
    b. Refine his/her delivery to suit the audience
    c. Not worry about attending the session on time

7. To a certain degree, public speakers can influence how their speaking environment is going to be: whether it is calm and quiet or noisy and disturbing.
    a. True
    b. False

8. Which of these two modes of presentation is more interactive and collaborative in nature?
    a. Webinar
    b. Virtual presentation

9. Why is it important for public speakers to engage in lifelong self-education and improvement?
    a. To learn new approaches for delivering their high-impact speeches
    b. To understand the slang or jargon spoken by their audience
    c. To be able to appear highly educated to his/her audience

10. **Which of these attitudes is expected of a professional public speaker?**
    a. Adaptable
    b. Arrogant
    c. Indifference

Answer key				
1 – c	2 – a	3 – b	4 – a	5 – b
6 – b	7 – a	8 – a	9 – a	10 – a

CHAPTER 12

Summarizing and Ending the Speech

Key Learning Objectives

- Learn how to summarize key takeaways
- Understand how to explain the last message
- Explore the different ways of ending on a high note

Have you heard the term "crescendo" in music?

It's when your words still echo even if you have stopped speaking or singing. Public speaking is all about providing a powerful ending to your presentation.

As a public speaker, your last message(s) must likewise be memorable and impactful.

For me, what worked beautifully is a powerful quote, a shocking statistic, a personal story, and a thought-provoking question.

This chapter explains how a public speaker can end their speeches in a way that their audience will respect their presentations and possibly request more.

12.1 Summarizing Key Takeaways

In public speaking, the final summary carries great weight. The moment of recap can also be considered a useful reinforcement of your message. A great summary weaves all the main points together and helps the audience understand them better. Make and clarify what exactly the speaker is trying to say.[60]

Summarizing isn't just a repeat of what has already been said; it's strategically designed to leave an impact on the audience so that every concept leads to one last, remembered takeaway. Some of the techniques listed below have various practical ways of constructing summaries. Speakers can customize them to suit their unique approaches.

12.1.1 Techniques for Summarizing

By mastering summary techniques, a speaker's impact can be elevated and change complex ideas into something clear and powerful. The following are the effective methods of summarizing a speech:

1. **Repetition:** Repetition is a powerful communication tool that great speakers often use to their advantage. They usually repeat the main keywords or ideas in their speeches for the purpose of firmly registering them in their audiences' minds. Human beings can generally internalize or easily remember things that they hear over and over again. By utilizing repetitions, speakers aim to help their audience's memory in a way that they can quickly recall what they have already been taught. Skillful speakers will mention their speeches' keywords or main ideas at the beginning, briefly make

---

60. Clella Jaffe, *Public Speaking: Concepts and Skills for a Diverse Society* (Cengage, 2015), 70-82.

a reference to them in the middle, and cleverly return to them while concluding their speeches.

One of my best speeches, which people still remember till today, had the title *"High to Low, Fast and Slow."*

After every paragraph of my story, I kept on saying, "High to Low, Fast and Slow," and at the end, having the audience repeat the message with me was a big success.

| Figure 12.1 | Benefits of Repetitions |

Repetition
- Repetition can help ensure your audience takes the main points away from your presentation.
- It promotes clarity and helps to encourage acceptance of an idea.
- In order to employ repetition in your presentations, determine what you want your audience to take away from your speech. Say it. Say it again.
  And then say it a third time just in case anyone missed it the first couple of times.

(Adapted from Azan Ali, 2025)[61]

2. **Listing the main points:** Listing the main points in a simple, bullet-point format has always been particularly effective. Such numbered or listed summaries are a structured overview that makes it easier for the listeners to digest. Likewise, during the conclusion of a speech on, say, *"the three core principles*

---

61. "Making Effective Oral Presentations", Azan Ali, accessed 15 June, 2025, https://www. slideshare.net/slideshow/making-effective-oral-presentations/226682250

of leadership," the speaker can reiterate *"Integrity, Accountability, Empathy"* to highlight the importance of these leadership attributes. This method offers clarity and helps the listeners to easily remember each point one by one.

3. **Simplifying Complex Ideas:** Summarization is a time to simplify. Breaking down complex ideas into simple, understandable language allows your audience to keep up with you without getting lost in the details or verbiage. If a presentation discusses technical technicalities, the speaker can explain, in simple terms, some complex descriptions using words everyone can understand. Simplifying things doesn't necessarily mean eliminating some important points from what you are sharing, but rather turning it into something that more people can grasp. By cutting out the jargon and using language everyone can comprehend, the speaker makes sure everyone clearly gets their message.

4. **Using Metaphors and Analogies:** Utilize metaphors and analogies when communicating abstract ideas to allow the other person to be grounded in what you are saying. So, if someone is giving a speech about resilience, he/she can end it by saying, *"Just as your muscles get stronger over time when you push them, so does your ability to be resilient as you are challenged."* This imagery explains the fundamentals of the topic, making it easier to be remembered and absorbed. Analogies that are well chosen can make abstract ideas feel relatable and help the audience remember the central idea through mental visualization.

5. **Summarizing with a Story:** Stories engage and relate, providing a long-lasting impact on the minds of your audience. To recap via a narrative, the speaker may

share an example brought up during the earlier part of the speech and revolve back to the key aspects. Circle the story back to the main points. So, if the speaker started with a challenge they faced relating to the topics in their talk and how they overcame that challenge, then in their summary, they could tie that back together to show some important lessons from that experience. This technique provides a sense of closure and, interestingly, reinforces the message in an engaging way that sticks.

12.1.2 Types of Key Takeaways

In a well-structured speech, the takeaways should reflect something that resonates with the audience's values, needs, or motivations. There are three broad classes of takeaways that a speech delivers, and each kind is different. By knowing these types, speakers can get a sense of how to orient the content of their summaries to meet audience expectations and end on a high note.

1. **Knowledge-Based Takeaways:** The emphasis with these takeaways is on knowledge and comprehension. This type is especially relevant in educational or informative speeches where the goal is to provide information to the audience. So, in an *"environment sustainability talk,"* an example of a knowledge-based takeaway would be learning that *"some small changes in lifestyle decrease carbon footprints significantly."* To emphasize this point, the speaker may offer three simple but effective steps the audience could take, such as reducing waste, conserving water, and taking public transport. This recap reiterates a few of those pieces of information already highlighted in the speech, ensuring the audience remembers all critical information.

2. **Emotional Takeaways:** Emotional takeaways create a strong feeling that remains long after the speech has ended. These tend to be the common outcomes or experiences from attending motivational or inspirational speeches, whereby the goal is to incite passion, emotional connection, or preach perseverance. As an example, if this speech is about resilience, the words to evoke emotional takeaway in the audience might be a statement that *"every setback is a setup for a comeback."* A summary like this targets the emotion of the audience and uses lingo that relates them to their personal experience or feeling. Vivid language, personal anecdotes, or quotes are frequent components of positive emotional takeaways that make the message resonate strongly with audiences.

3. **Actionable Takeaways:** An action-oriented takeaway is designed to move the audience toward a course of behavior, action, or change. These are typical of persuasive speeches or any other form of advocacy where the main objective is to get the audience to take some specific actions. The speaker can conclude by challenging the audience to undertake a change, like volunteering, adopting new habits, or supporting certain causes. For example, when encouraging reading, a speaker can initiate an action-oriented takeaway by calling the audience to read one book a month. Another way would be to create action by taking a 30-day challenge on the same. This type of takeaway makes such a speech a catalyst for action.

TIP

Putting It All Together: Writing a Comprehensive Summary

The most effective summaries incorporate the following techniques and encourage the audience to leave the event venues with different takeaway types:

1. **Conclude by restating key points:** Use listing or repetition to briefly remind the audience of each key point.

2. **Metaphor or Story:** Add a metaphor or story that may connect the dots in driving home the theme of the message.

3. **Powerful Takeaway:** Conclude powerfully and let your audience go home with the knowledge-based, emotive, or action-oriented takeaways as related to the purpose of your speech.

12.1.3 Crafting an Emotional Message

One of the practical ways speakers can leave a lasting emotional impact on their audience is to link personal insights with inspiration. This is achieved through sincere speech, personal anecdotes, or even pathos-laden rhetoric. When well executed, an emotional message is capable of turning even passive listeners into active reflectors. Here are some approaches for constructing a powerful and memorable emotional message:

1. **Use Personal Stories for Authenticity:** The effectiveness of personal stories comes from the authenticity, gravity, and meaning that personal stories bring to

the speaker's words. By sharing an instance from one's life, speakers are allowed to show the relevance of a message in such a way that makes sense to their audience. For example, if a speech is on resilience, speakers may discuss a time when they faced extreme adversity but came out of it stronger. Make it like a "hero's story."

Personal stories create a direct emotional bond whereby the audience feels the speaker is not just uttering theoretical principles but has actually lived and breathed through them. For a story to be powerfully told, it needs to be honest, relevant, and communicated in a manner that invites the audience into the experience of the speaker.

2. **Employ Inspirational Language:** The choice of language is a critical aspect of every emotionally appealing message. Words that are vivid, direct, and emotionally charged can tremendously stir the audience's feelings. Inspirational language relies on simple yet powerful words combined with dynamic phrasing to persuade the audience to look at the world in a different way. Instead, the speaker could say, *"There is a strength within you that has not been tapped."* Notice that the statement does not only say that one should believe in oneself, but it also sparks curiosity as one wonders what is inside oneself. With a careful choice of words that speak to human aspirations, tussles, and dreams, speakers can frame their messages in such a way as to actually connect with their audience on an emotional level.

3. **Include Memorable Quotations:** A well-chosen quote can reveal the power of a speech if it's linked to the theme and beautifully delivered. Quotes by respected individuals, like "Be the change you wish to see in the world" by Mahatma Gandhi, can impart to the

audience a sense of wisdom and gravity. A personal quote, even a phrase that a speaker has coined themselves, may provide a unique take on giving an original zest to the speech. The chosen quote should be relevant, supporting the message of the speech in such a way that it will easily stick in the minds of the audience.

4. **Ask a Reflective Question:** Rhetorical questions are powerful because they engage the audience's brains and cause them to reflect. A question placed well at the end of a speech invites listeners to think about how the topic can help them in their personal or professional lives. For example, if the speech was about achieving success, the speaker might say, *"What would you do if you knew you couldn't fail?"* Such a question provides a moment of pause in which listeners must momentarily stop and muse. Thus, a question engages hearers in considering new possibilities or in re-evaluating personal ambitions. Rhetorical questions serve especially well as concluding messages because they transform inactive listeners into active thinkers, motivating them to take the speech message and put it to work in their lives.

5. **Provide a Call to Action:** Concluding with a call to action is one of the most common methods of closing a persuasive or inspirational type of speaking. By calling on the audience to take an action, whether to change something in their lives, volunteer, or consider a new way of thinking, the speech's message systematically transitions into an action. In a speech about environmental awareness, the speaker may conclude by saying, *"Let's each commit to one small action today that will make a difference for our planet."* Calls to action urge audiences not simply to think about something

but to do something about what they have been told. But the action must be appropriate and relevant to the speech theme.

6. **Use Poetic Language and Rhythm:** Rhythm and poetic language can elevate the last message, making it memorable and pleasing to the ear. For example, repetition of a phrase can create a cadence that gives the final words weight. A speaker might say, *"Together, we can change. Together, we can build. Together, we are unstoppable."* The rhythm in these statements creates a sense of unity and momentum, reinforcing the speech's message with emotional intensity. Additionally, alliteration, rhyme, or parallel structure can lend a lyrical quality, making the words easier to remember and more enjoyable to listen to. Poetic language can add a layer of artistry to the message, enhancing its impact.

12.2 Last Message

Every speaker must conclude their speeches by offering their last messages. Here are some approaches any speaker can adopt in crafting his/her last message:

Let's see how to create an unforgettable last message!

1. **Let it be the core message:** The final message should be a reflection of the main theme or argument that knitted the whole speech together in one short message. For example, a speech about overcoming challenges could conclude with, *"Remember, every obstacle you experience is one more step to the strength you build."*

2. **Keep it concise:** The backbone of any powerful last message is brevity. A few well-chosen words can be more poignant than a whole paragraph. A concise message is also more easily remembered by your audience and is easy to apply in their lives.

3. **Create emotional resonance:** Find those words that touch the feelings of the audience—be it hope, courage, oneness, or sympathy. You want to reach them at their cores and make them feel your presence. What people feel definitely leaves an imprint that extends beyond the speech moment.

4. **Practice delivery:** Even the most inspiring words can lose their impact if not delivered with conviction. Pausing, using varied tones, and making eye contact can amplify the emotional gravity of the message, helping it land on the minds of your audience with authenticity.

5. **End with confidence:** The way a speaker finishes his/her speech communicates as much as the words themselves. A firm, self-confident delivery conveys belief, leaving the audience with a sense of certainty and motivation.

Figure 12.2 Ending the speech with confidence

Confidence
- A highly confident presentator is viewed as being more accurate, competent, credible, intelligent, knowledgeable, likable, and believable than the less confident uncertain presentator.
- When it comes to public speaking, confidence is key (not the only key mind you). When speaking in public, it's only natural to be nervous.

(Source: Azan Ali, 2025)[62]

---

62. "Making Effective Oral Presentations, Azan Ali, accessed 4 June, 2025, "https://www.slideshare.net/slideshow/making-effective-oral-presentations/226682250

12.3 Ending on a High Note

Closing a speech on a high note is a rhetorical strategy that amplifies the message, re-energizes the audience, and engraves the message in their minds. When speakers make a concluding statement with a note of positivity, hope, or inspiration, they don't just end a speech, but they leave something to be forever remembered by their audience long after they have gone their separate ways. A high-note ending capitalizes on emotional appeal through captivating tone, narrative, and elocution-laden speech that calls up emotion in joy, hope, or collective mission.

12.3.1 Approaches to High-Note Endings

Indeed, to deliver a memorable speech, stir emotion, inspire optimism, and genuinely connect with their audience, speakers can adopt these three effective ways to close their speeches on a high note:

1. **Anecdotal impact:** A well-chosen anecdote is a great way of leaving with impact, as one drives home the message. And the audience will be emotionally touched.

2. **Positive tone:** Concluding with a message of hope and optimism sends off the audience inspired and energized. The uplifting language, aspirational ideas, and vision for a better future can instill positivity and confidence in the audience.

3. **Closing with thankfulness/gratitude:** Thankfulness is something that immediately resonates with people on a deeper level, evoking warm, feel-good, and inclusive feelings. When speakers thank the audience after their speeches, they make the audience feel valued and appreciated, because gratitude can unite individuals

across the board in a very touching and moving manner.

> **TIP**

Tips for Practicing a Powerful Finish

Writing a high-note closing statement is one thing; delivering it well is what makes it shine. Practice and timing are the key elements of a strong closing. Here are a few tips that need to be considered when planning to deliver a speech ending on a high note:

1. **Practice with a Purpose:** The conclusion should be practiced in a way that each word is spoken well and clearly with confidence, placing emphasis on certain words or phrases.

2. **Pause for Emphasis:** Learn how to strategically pause while delivering a high-note ending because it will make your closing powerful.

3. **Control the Tone and Energy:** Speakers must control their voices to convey the desired emotions to the audience, whether hope, excitement, or gratitude.

4. **Make Eye Contact:** At the end of the day, eye contact is what demonstrates sincerity and respect to the audience.

5. **Conclude with Confidence and Poise:** Public speakers need to be confident while delivering their speech, using appropriate body language and postures.

Chapter Summary

- Summarizing the takeaways from a speech at its closing can draw the audience to the most important aspects of the speech content—its main takeaways.

- Interestingly enough, the audience usually derives three key takeaways from every speech: emotional takeaway, actionable takeaway, and knowledge-based takeaway.

- Public speakers' last messages are as important as their main speeches. This is why they should make their last statements strong and memorable.

- Through regular practice and self-development in their profession, public speakers can definitely master how to end their speeches on a high note, in a way that their audience can quickly recall them.

Quiz

1. Public speakers are expected to be confident while delivering their final message, using appropriate body language and postures.
   a. False
   b. True

2. Ms. Danielle and Ms. Mary are both public speakers. Who do you think did a good job preparing and practicing their speeches before they delivered them? Considering that Ms. Danielle finished her presentation with a strong, emotional ending that deeply connected with her audience, while Ms. Mary's speech closing was weak and not-well-thought-through?
   a. Ms. Mary
   b. Ms. Danielle

3. Which of these statements is NOT true about public speaking?
   a. Naturally gifted speakers don't need to prepare and practice their speeches
   b. Giving a speech's summary helps the audience to recap the core points
   c. Having a weak ending to a speech reveals a lack of adequate preparation

4. Which of the following is NOT a technique recommended for summarizing a speech?
   a. Repetition
   b. Listing the main points
   c. Asking the audience some questions

5. When summarizing a speech with a story, it is advisable to _____ .

   a. Tell a story related to the speech's topic
   b. Tell a story that is not related to the speech
   c. A story that the audience may have a hard time understanding

6. Professional speakers can choose to use metaphors and analogies to end their speeches.

   a. False
   b. True

7. When the audience gains new ideas/information and understanding after attending a speech is often referred to as _____ .

   a. Actionable takeaways
   b. Knowledge-based takeaways
   c. Emotional takeaways

8. Sometimes, the audience leaves a meeting venue crying and energized; this can be referred to as _____ .

   a. Emotional takeaways
   b. Knowledge-based takeaways
   c. Actionable takeaways

9. Many labor union meetings and human rights campaigns cause the audience to take a definite action, such as going on a protest or picketing their employers. This is a typical example of _____ .

   a. Emotional takeaways
   b. Actionable takeaways
   c. Knowledge-based takeaways

10. Public speakers can conclude their speeches strongly by briefly restating, listing, or repeating each key point in their speeches.

    a. True

    b. False

Answer Key

1 – b	2 – b	3 – a	4 – c	5 – a
6 – b	7 – b	8 – a	9 – b	10 – a

CHAPTER 13

Public Speaking As A Viable Platform—My Toastmasters Journey

Key Learning Objectives

- Identifying internal motivators
- Understanding the journey to becoming a successful public speaker
- Learning beyond Toastmasters: A message to every speaker
- Reframing negative affirmations into positive ones

In this chapter, I invite you on a heartfelt journey—one that traces my transformation from a quiet, hesitant speaker to a confident, in-demand voice on stage.

Today, I'm humbled to be recognized with several awards and regularly invited by top corporations and organizations to deliver powerful keynotes, conduct skill-driven workshops, and give motivational talks.

But it wasn't always this way. I began as the exact opposite of who I am now—shy, soft-spoken, and gripped by stage fright. I was the girl who avoided the spotlight and kept her words to herself. I was always the last bencher.

What changed? How did I move from being that last bencher to being a front mentor?

I achieved this through intentional growth, consistent effort, and a deep desire to rise above my fears. Through purposeful practice and preparation, I redefined myself—and if I can do it, so can you!

This chapter is your proof that confident public speaking isn't a gift for a select few—it's a skill that can be learned, shaped, and mastered.

13.1 There Is Something About You, Ami!

The flight landed in Mumbai.

After spending a decade in China with a successful training career, I returned to India—a country I loved—with a heart full of dreams and a 2-year-old toddler in tow. What I didn't anticipate was the storm I would face after moving to India: postnatal depression, a career sabbatical, and an overwhelming shift from a nuclear setup to a full-blown joint family. In those days of self-doubt and silent tears, a voice inside me would scream:

"There is *nothing* about you, Ami. Nothing."

Can you relate?

Then I knocked, literally, on the door of the Powai Toastmasters Club.

At first, I visited like many guests do—curious and unsure. But I found something unexpected: a platform to vent, a pathway to grow, and a supportive tribe that said, "We see you. We hear you." A public speaking experiential learning platform! The biggest shift was when I took those baby steps and actions to come and speak in public.

What is Toastmasters?[63] Toastmasters International is a global non-profit organization that provides a safe and supportive environment to practice public speaking and acquire important leadership and communication skills. By paying a very nominal fee, you can join a local club and expose yourself to structured mentorships that can gradually improve your confidence and charisma by executing some assigned projects and roles relating to public speaking.

13.2 Journey to Becoming A Successful Public Speaker

13.2.1 The Icebreaker That Broke the Ice

My official journey began with the Icebreaker speech. Imagine a hall filled with 60+ people as Tata Consultancy Services (TCS) and Powai Toastmasters merged for a mega meet. My hands were cold, my script shaky, but I poured my heart into a story titled *"Last Bencher to Front Mentor."*

And when I finished, there was a standing ovation. Distinguished Toastmaster (DTM) Mukta walked up to me and said, "You have storytelling magic."

That one moment shifted something in me forever.

Confidence. Clarity. Charisma!

---

63. *Toastmasters International is a nonprofit educational organization that builds confidence and teaches public speaking skills through a worldwide network of clubs that meet online and in person. In a supportive community or corporate environment, members prepare and deliver speeches, respond to impromptu questions, and give and receive constructive feedback. It is through this regular practice that members are empowered to meet personal and professional communication goals. Founded in 1924, the organization is headquartered in Englewood, Colorado with approximately 270,000 members in more than 14,000 clubs in 150 countries.*

That's what Toastmasters gave me—and it can give you, too.

What makes it magical is how an ordinary Saturday morning or a quiet weekday evening transforms into a stage—a real one.

You don't just speak—you perform, evaluate, get feedback, and evolve—one speech at a time.

Whether you're just starting out or already commanding rooms, Toastmasters meets you where you are and takes you higher.

I still remember my next speech.

It was a humorous contest piece titled "Toddler's Mom." It's still on my YouTube channel if you'd like to watch it.

That day, I didn't perform—I shared.

Raw. Real. From the heart.

The audience laughed, clapped, and leaned in.

Someone even asked, "Where are you from? You speak from your heart!"

And that's when a whisper inside me said: "Ami, there's something about you."

And what's that something?

It was the speaker within, finally coming alive.

I based my second speech on the revisions and feedback received from my first speech.

The next speech was on great vocal variety, but then the lockdown happened. Now here is when I spoke about the *how, what,* and *when* of COVID-19 lockdowns. The speech was titled "My Lockdown Diary" and delivered online due to the lockdown. Through this project, I learned how to systematically prepare and deliver a speech online, which turned out to be an exhilarating moment for me. Speech was again part of a humorous contest and went from the club to the area-level win.

I still remember one of the most impactful speeches I worked on during the lockdown. It was a project that required research and delivery—two skills I was eager to master. I chose to speak on a topic close to my heart: the benefits of waking up early. I titled my speech "The 5 AM Club," drawing inspiration from Robin Sharma's[64] book but going beyond that with data, research insights, and my personal experiences.

During the lockdown, I had made it a habit to wake up at 5 AM. Those early hours became my sacred time, filled with clarity, productivity, and purpose. In my speech, I shared how that routine transformed my energy levels, mindset, and focus.

What made this speech stand out wasn't just the content—it was the connection I built with the audience. Even though it was delivered online, the stories, analytics, and persuasive elements resonated deeply. The feedback I received was overwhelming. Many told me it inspired them to reflect on their morning routines and take action.

That experience taught me a powerful lesson: when you blend research with personal stories, you don't just inform—you inspire.

Thereafter, I participated in a speech contest where the speech title was "High to low, fast and Slow." It was one of my personal stories that explained how I survived pneumonia during my time in China and all the stages of my life when I was high to low, fast and slow. It was a winning

---

64. Robin, Sharma, *The 5AM Club: Own Your Morning. Elevate Your Life.* (HarperCollins, 2020), 20.

speech for the international speech contest from the club to the area to division-level contest as a runner-up.

13.2.2 From Stage Fright to Spotlight

By aligning myself with this public speaking club, I was able to acquire new skills and master my existing ones. These skills included communication skills, public speaking, leadership, and more.

The experience gave me structure as an emerging public speaker. It exposed me to the concepts of crafting my speech, time management, structuring my thoughts, and getting better and better on the stage. It was quite exhilarating learning how to prepare, perform, and reflect on speeches I was delivering during my formative periods. I gained my very first corporate training assignment with TISS (Tata Institute of Social Science) just by networking at this club. That singular experience opened the doors to several high-paying training gigs and opportunities later in my career as a corporate trainer.

13.2.3 Reigniting the Fire After a Break

There was a time when I felt I needed a break due to my hectic schedule and other issues.

Post-break, I returned to the Toastmasters club with more powerful and connecting speeches while restarting my career as a corporate trainer.

Stepping out of my comfort zone, I delivered a program on *Emotional Intelligence and conflict resolution* to the senior leaders of the organization. And I was elated to receive rave reviews and applause after the program was completed.

The praises kept ringing in my ears: *"There is something about you, Ami."*

This may have happened because before every training, I would convert it into speech and practice it at the Toastmasters Club.

13.2.4 Refined Techniques and Real-World Practice

As I progressed in my Toastmasters journey, my speeches kept getting better day by day, week after week, going from excellent to phenomenal. That was the candid feedback I had received from my mentors year after year. The perks of being part of this club were receiving awards and gaining confidence.

In this journey, I mastered some great speaking tools like

- Starting my speeches with powerful quotes and questions
- Creating audience engagement
- Adding strong voice modulation techniques
- The power of body language

I soon figured out that speaking professionally can happen after some periods of personal transformation. After all this time, my strategic thinking capability has improved tremendously, and I can deliver a high-level presentation with minimal preparation.

On one occasion, with zero preparation, I stood up to deliver a powerful speech titled *"Being a Confident Communicato*r" —an 18-minute keynote speech using transcendence, pauses, and purpose.

People said, "Ami, *you're TED-ready. We get inspired by you.*" This time around, the applause grew louder and the whisper grew louder: *"There is something about you, Ami!"*

All of this happened just because I took actions, and those actions worked because I had belief in myself.

13.3 Beyond Toastmasters: A Message to Every Speaker

My sincere advice to all the readers is to find a platform, and if you don't have one, create it! Would you like to know how?

Assuming you are attending your best friend's wedding, even though you are not the official Master of Ceremonies (MC), take a moment to get in front of the guests and briefly address them. You could be telling some old jokes about your best friend or wholeheartedly thanking the guests for attending the party.

If you are having a family get-together, stand up and say something to the people—maybe a short story or joke, or some fun element about your past.

If you are a student who is always labelled as an introvert, get out of your comfort zone and participate in college festivals.

You don't need a perfect stage: I found this public speaking platform, but if I hadn't, I would have created one for myself. So can you. When I had no platform and I had moved to a country like China, I learned some things about the culture of the country and the people. And despite not knowing the language, I spoke to the people and won their hearts by running English corners for them on the university campus.

"Opportunities Are Everywhere"

I come from the last bench, and every step that I have taken, from getting rejected in interviews to winning awards for my speeches, I have had that strong mindset to take advantage of every opportunity that I have come across. I've stumbled, hesitated, and been overlooked. But every time, I chose to show up. Every rejection, every stumble, every tiny opportunity—I took it and turned it into a stepping stone. By doing the same, you will get a lot of opportunities. Opportunities are just around you, and all you need to do is grab them.

Don't let the past, limiting beliefs, hold you back. Don't stay stuck in the negative affirmations like:

"I'm scared."

"I'm not good enough as a speaker."

"He or she is better than I."

Instead, try saying this to yourself:

"I'm willing to try."

"I'm ready to grow."

"I will speak up—even if my voice shakes."

You don't need permission. You need a decision.

Move from that fixed ideology to a growth mindset. Because I decided to build a mindset, not of fear, but of **growth.** A mindset that says:

"I may not be the best yet, but 'Every day in every way I am getting better and better.'" This is my favorite affirmation that I like to repeat to myself.

Remember, your voice deserves to be heard.

And the world is waiting for your message.

Chapter Summary

- "There Is Something About You, Ami!" became the internal motivator that got Speaker Ami energized to the point of overcoming her previous fear and self-doubt, becoming the powerful public speaker she is today. The moral lesson is to identify your internal motivator, the specific phrase or words that often inspire you to strive harder and achieve all your life goals!

- The author's Toastmasters journey reveals a life of dedication and consistent willingness to take all the necessary risks in researching, preparing, delivering, and polishing her speeches. Nothing ever happens by chance, and Speaker Ami has demonstrated this fact with concrete and relatable examples.

- A powerful reminder for readers to move away from negative affirmations in their lives and turn to positive affirmations for a growth mindset.

A Speaker's Spotlight

Eloquence 2025—Meeting A Legend

One of the defining moments of my Toastmasters journey came at *Eloquence 2025*, held in the Pink City of Jaipur. That's where I met **Mark Brown**, the 1995 World Champion of Public Speaking.

Mark's presence lit up the stage. His deep voice, natural storytelling, emotional range, and message delivery showed what true mastery looks like. His winning speech, *"A Second Chance,"* is still watched by millions because it is authentic, heartfelt, and powerful. What makes Mark a world champion isn't just technique—it's the *truth* he brings to his words.

Insights from the Master

As you advance in your public speaking career, cultivate the habit of mingling with other speakers, some of whom you can learn one or two tricks of the trade from. I have had mentors and cheerleaders throughout my journey. All speakers learn something about public speaking from one another in a creative manner.

Here is an exclusive interview I had with **1995 World Champion of Public Speaking Mark Brown**. I sincerely hope you will learn, from this interview, what it *really* takes to grab your audience's attention in the first 30 seconds, overcome stage fright, use your voice and silence like a pro, and turn your captivating stories into impact.

Transcript: Interview with Mark Brown—World Champion of Public Speaking, 1995.

Hi, everyone, this is Ami Ved from Speak with Ami, and I'm thrilled to bring you a special conversation with Mr. Mark Brown, the 1995 World Champion of Public Speaking. We met at Eloquence 2025 in Jaipur, and I had the honor of asking him key questions about his journey, mindset, and secrets to becoming a powerful speaker.

Ami: Mark, what was the turning point that led you into the world of public speaking?

Mark: I was inspired by my uncle, the late Courtney Orr, who was Jamaica's first Toastmaster and a Supreme Court judge. He introduced the program to Jamaica in the mid-80s. Years later, I saw a Toastmasters pin while working at Reader's Digest in New York. That connection inspired me to join Toastmasters. If it worked for him, I believed it could work for me too, and that was the beginning of my journey.

Ami: Many struggle with mindset and inner communication. What's one mindset shift that helped you move from a good to a world-class communicator?

Mark: One powerful shift is understanding the importance of cross-generational and cross-cultural communication. We now live in a world where different generations and cultures must interact daily. The real skill is mastering human, one-on-one communication. AI won't replace that. This mindset empowers you to connect across age, race, and culture.

Ami: What made your 1995 World Championship speech stand out?

Mark: My speech addressed a universal theme—how we treat those who are different. It's sad but true that this topic is still relevant today. The speech has stood the test of time because it appeals to the human condition. The key is crafting a message with relevance, impact, and emotional resonance.

Ami: Stage fear is very common. How do you handle nervousness?

👤 **Mark:** Nerves usually come from lack of preparation. If you're well-prepared and approach the stage with the mindset of 'I get to do this,' then the fear shifts into eagerness. Also, fear isn't about speaking—it's about being judged. But audiences are rooting for you. They want you to succeed.

👤 **Ami:** What are your top 3 tips for someone new to public speaking?

👤 **Mark:**

1. Be crystal clear on your message—know what you want to say.

2. Use personal stories to support that message—your life is full of relatable experiences.

3. Structure your speech—start strong, deliver the main idea, support it, and end with a clear call to action.

👤 **Ami:** How can one structure their thoughts better when speaking?

👤 **Mark:** Write down what you want the audience to remember. Focus on one big idea, especially in short speeches. Don't overwhelm with too many points. Sequence your thoughts logically. It takes practice, but it's worth it.

👤 **Ami:** How has public speaking transformed your life?

👤 **Mark:** I was a mainframe computer programmer before winning the championship. Toastmasters changed my life. I became a full-time speaker and coach. But I never stopped learning—every day brings new lessons, even for world champions.

👤 **Ami:** Any advice for someone beginning their journey in communication?

👤 **Mark:** Join Toastmasters if you can—it's global and transformative. Also, read books, watch TED Talks, and listen to podcasts. I co-wrote 'Deliver Unforgettable Presentations' and host a free podcast with over 300 episodes. Learn from good speakers, but most importantly, keep practicing and growing. The voice of reason, influence, and leadership starts with communication.

Thank you so much, Mark. This conversation has been rich in insights and full of encouragement.

To all readers: build your skill, refine your message, and become the confident communicator the world needs.

You can watch the entire interview by scanning the below given QR code:

Bibliography

"100 Years of Communication Excellence." Toastmasters International, accessed 10 December, 2024. https://www.toastmasters.org/

"13 July 1934 - Adolf Hitler-Speech to the Reichstag," n.d. https://www.der-fuehrer.org/reden/english/34-07-13.htm.

Acker, Mike, *Speak With No Fear: Go From a Nervous, Nauseated, and Sweaty Speaker to an Excited, Energized, and Passionate Presenter* (Advance, Coaching and Consulting, 2019), 65–78, https://www.amazon.in/Speak-Fear-nauseated-energized-passionate/dp/1733980008.

Aristotle and Robert Bartlett, Aristotle's Art of Rhetoric (Chicago, Chicago University Press, 2021), 70-72.

Borthwick, Derek, *Body Language How to Read Any Body - the Secret to Nonverbal Communication to Understand & Influence in, Business, Sales, Online, Presenting & Public Speaking, Healthcare, Attraction & Seduction,* 2022, 102–33, https://www.amazon.in/Body-Language-How-Read-Communication/dp/1838334629.

Clella Iles Jaffe, *Public Speaking: Concepts and Skills for a Diverse Society,* 8th ed., 2016, 70–82, https://www.cengage.com/c/public-speaking-concepts-and-skills-for-a-diverse-society-8e-jaffe/9781285445854/.

DeGeorgia, Michael, 2001,"Public Speaking Anxiety," National Social Anxiety Center. https://nationalsocialanxietycenter.com/social-anxiety/public-speaking-anxiety/#:~:text=The%20fear%20of%20public%20speaking%20is%20the%20most,fear%20is%20judgment%20or%20negative%20evaluation%20by%20others.

Doumont, Jean-Luc. Trees, Maps, and Theorems: Effective Communication for Rational Minds. Principiae, 2009.

Duarte, Nancy, *Resonate: Present Visual Stories That Transform Audiences* (Wiley, 2010), 57, https://www.amazon.in/Resonate-Present-Stories-Transform-Audiences/dp/0470632011/ref=sr_1_1?adgrpid=61741835187&dib=eyJ2IjoiMSJ9.H9MASFYOs9Oks8lc_pSYGN14jPakQK7TFzWlxgEA56bIPr_QJjFMzGQI_l0-dTP8RYwYG969XNYit8lv2ppTEQYVpgWSouhFFJZKd ch8THDxrKk3IY6kwKJ9C4VncQxuD6KXGHmkyI7R2ZTXhLaXyQ.6xV UzPKWhd--m6_6hvUAhpn21P-Scu5Rbp78uxdVzUY&dib_tag=se&ext_vrnc=hi&hvadid=590331320775&hvdev=c&hvlocphy=9199116&hvnetw=g&hvqmt=e&hvrand=9083653919206734951&hvtargid=kwd-311007855745&hydadcr=8214_2244729&keywords=resonate+by+nancy+duarte&mcid=4bc526c14c1039ebb6fa9cbcdffaa1fe&qid=1754283391&sr=8-1.

ESPN. "LeBron James Says He Can Still Give the Game Everything |
2023 ESPYS (❯ @CapitalOne)," July 13, 2023. https://www.youtube.com/
watch?v=YonmfL9GvOw.

Hale, John R., *The Art of Public Speaking: Lessons From the Greatest Speeches in
History* (The Great Courses, 2010), 28–45, https://www.amazon.in/Art-Public-
Speaking-Greatest-Speeches/dp/1598037013.

Hallsby, Atilla. "Chapter 2: The 'Origins' of Rhetorical Theory." Reading
Rhetorical Theory, n.d. https://open.lib.umn.edu/rhetoricaltheory/chapter/
origins-of-rhetorical-theory/.

Harvard Professional & Executive Development. "10 Tips for Improving Your
Public Speaking Skills". https://professional.dce.harvard.edu/blog/10-tips-for-
improving-your-public-speaking-skills/

Huang, Zhao Alexandre, China's Public Diplomacy and Confucius Institute,
Public Diplomacy and the Politics of Uncertainty, In press, 10.1007/978-3-030-
54552-9_8 . hal-02910002

King Jr., Martin Luther, *I Have a Dream: Writings and Speeches That Changed the
World*, ed. James M. Washington (HarperOne, n.d.), 56–88, https://www.amazon.
in/Have-Dream-Writings-Speeches-Changed/dp/0062505521.

Luna, Wilson. "Your Words Only Tell a Fraction of the Story — Here's
Why Tone and Body Language Actually Matter More." Entrepreneur,
February 27, 2025. https://www.entrepreneur.com/leadership/
your-words-only-tell-a-fraction-of-the-story-heres-why/485004.

McGarrity, Matt, Introduction to Public Speaking (Coursera, 2025). https://www.
coursera.org/instructor/mcgarrity

National Geographic. "Jason Silva's Origin Story | Origins: The
Journey of Humankind," March 15, 2017. https://www.youtube.com/
watch?v=peXVGSGllvo.

S, Pangambam. "Steve Jobs: How to Live Before You Die 2005 Speech (Full
Transcript)." The Singju Post, August 16, 2023. https://singjupost.com/
steve-jobs-how-to-live-before-you-die-2005-speech-full-transcript/.

Segal, Jeanne, PhD, Melinda Smith MA, Lawrence Robinson, and Greg Boose.
"Body Language and Nonverbal Communication." HelpGuide.Org (blog),
March 13, 2025. https://www.helpguide.org/relationships/communication/
nonverbal-communication.

Sharma, Robin, The 5 AM Club: Own Your Morning. Elevate Your Life.
(HarperCollins, 2020), 20.

Sinek, Simon, "Start with why -- how great leaders inspire action | Simon Sinek | TEDxPugetSound". Microsoft Bing. https://www.bing.com/videos/riverview/relatedvideo?q=noting+that+Simon+Sinek%2c+in+his+Start+with+Why+TED+Talk&mid=98A8E88B256F2759A00298A8E88B256F2759A002&FORM=VIRE

Souers, Melinda. "Public Speaking: Getting Beyond the Fear Through the Three P's - UF/IFAS Extension Orange County." UF/IFAS Extension Orange County, February 1, 2022. https://blogs.ifas.ufl.edu/orangeco/2022/01/21/public-speaking-getting-beyond-the-fear-through-the-three-ps/.

TED. 2022. Bill Gates' TED talks. https://www.ted.com/speakers/bill_gates

TED.2010. David McCandless draws beautiful conclusions from complex datasets — thus revealing unexpected insights into our world. https://www.ted.com/speakers/david_mccandless

TEDX. 2015. Second Chances. https://www.youtube.com/watch?v=F2dFiK3wkR

Further Reading

1. **HBR's 10 Must Reads on Public Speaking and Presenting** – A collection of Harvard Business Review articles on mastering presentations and audience engagement

   http://bit.ly/465Q7Ii

2. **TED Talks: The Official TED Guide to Public Speaking** by Chris Anderson

3. **Confessions of a Public Speaker** by Scott Berkun

4. **Talk Like TED: The 9 Public-Speaking Secrets of the World's Top Minds** by Carmine Gallo

5. **Speak Like Churchill, Stand Like Lincoln** by James Hume

6. **Resonate: Present Visual Stories that Transform Audiences** by Nancy Duarte

7. **How to Develop Self-Confidence and Influence People by Public Speaking** by Dale Carnegie

8. **Win Every Argument: The Art of Debating, Persuading, and Public Speaking** by Mehdi Hasan

9. **The Successful Speaker** by Grant Baldwin

10. **How to Speak, How to Listen** by Mortimer J. Adler

NOTES

www.ingramcontent.com/pod-product-compliance
Lightning Source LLC
Chambersburg PA
CBHW050342270326
41926CB00016B/3572